STO

ALLEN COUNTY PUBLIC LIBRARY

ACPL IT P9-EDI-989

DISCARDED

About the Book

In Hindu legend, the Milky Way was the former bed of the Ganges River, one of the holy places of India. Ancient travelers who were superstitious thought that if the star Antares rose in the morning their trail would be dogged by robbers and thieves. Venus, the beautiful goddess of love, was once the goddess of the Roman sewers.

These are some of the fascinating and little-known facts that provide the basis for Peter Limburg's lively stories of the stars, planets and constellations. What the ancients believed and what scientists know today are related in excellent essays about the etymologies of more than fifty heavenly bodies and the astronomical terms. Carolyn Croll's humorous illustrations take up and enhance the light-hearted tone of the book.

WHAT'S IN THE NAMES OF

STARS AND

CONSTELLATIONS

BY PETER LIMBURG

ILLUSTRATED BY CAROLYN CROLL

COWARD, McCANN & GEOGHEGAN, INC. NEW YORK

To the scientists who made sense of the mysteries of the skies, and to the collectors of lore and legend on whose books I have drawn, this book is gratefully dedicated.

I would like to give special thanks to my consultant, Jerome Wyckoff, who, as a former boss, taught me much about the craft of writing and whose help has been invaluable with the scientific aspects of this book.

Text copyright © 1976 by Peter Limburg
Illustrations·copyright © 1976 by Carolyn Croll
All rights reserved. This book, or parts thereof, may not be reproduced in any form without permission in writing from the publishers. Published simultaneously in Canada by Longman Canada Limited, Toronto.
SBN: GB-698-30611-2   SBN: TR-698-20359-3

Library of Congress Cataloging in Publication Data

Limburg, Peter R
 What's in the names of stars and constellations.

 1. Stars—Names—Juvenile literature. 2. Constellations—Names—Juvenile literature. 3. Astronomy—Juvenile literature. I. Croll, Carolyn. II. Title.
QB802.L58   1976   523.8'01'42   76-13637

PRINTED IN THE UNITED STATES OF AMERICA

WHAT'S IN THE NAMES OF

STARS AND

CONSTELLATIONS

1935388

Star

Star comes from the Anglo-Saxon *steorra*, which goes back to an old Indo-European root that may have been *ster*. Some scholars think that the original word meant "strew" because the stars are strewn about the sky like a giant handful of lights. In case you are interested, the word for "star" in Greek is *aster*; in Latin, *stella*, from which come the French word *étoile* and the Spanish and Portuguese *estrella*; in German, *Stern*; in Swedish, *stjärna*, in Polish, *gwiazda*. In Hebrew it is *kochab*, and in Arabic *kaukab*.

Ancient peoples counted as stars anything that shone in the sky at night, including the moon and the planets and comets and meteors. Modern astronomers define a star as a body in space that shines by its own light. This lets out planets, and satellites, which shine with reflected light, and comets, which glow with the heat of friction as they rush through the atmosphere. Put another way, a star is another sun.

No one knows how many stars there are in the universe, but astronomers estimate that there are one hundred *billion* in our galaxy—the Milky Way—alone. To make this huge number more meaningful, imagine that you had a spaceship that could transport you instantly from star to star, using no time at all, and that you wanted to spend one second on each star. At this rate, it would take you 3,000 years to visit all the stars in the Milky Way. Multiply this by the billions of other galaxies that astronomers believe exist, and you will have an idea of the unimaginable numbers of stars.

A star is born from an immense, whirling cloud of gases and cosmic dust floating in space. Over millions of years, gravitational attraction pulls the gas and dust particles closer together. The closer they come, the more strongly they attract each other. Atoms and molecules collide with each other, and this releases heat. Eventually the center of the cloud mass becomes so hot that nuclear reactions begin to take place, slowly at first and then faster and faster as the star cloud continues to contract. Eventually these nuclear reactions (mostly hydrogen atoms being fused into helium) are powerful enough to counteract the star's gravitational force, and the star stops shrinking. After a very long time, the star uses up so much of its hydrogen "fuel" that it begins to shrink again. This sets in motion a complex chain of reactions. The end result is that the star burns so fiercely that it puffs up into a huge, relatively cool "red giant." After this, the dying star may explode in a last burst of energy, or it may shrink down to a dim "white dwarf." Eventually it will go cold and dark.

But star material is constantly being recycled. Matter given off by burning stars drifts through space and forms clouds that eventually become new stars. Our own sun may be a second- or third-generation star formed in this way.

The brightness of a star is measured in two ways. *Intrinsic* brightness is the amount of light the star produces. Stars are so far away, however, that only a tiny fraction of their light reaches earth. The light we see is called *apparent* brightness. A very distant star may produce fifty times as much light as a star closer to earth, but the nearby star may still appear brighter.

A star's apparent brightness is measured in *magnitudes*. (*Magnitude* has nothing to do with magnets. It is the Latin word for "greatness" or "size.") The magnitude scale is set up so that a first-magnitude star is brighter than a second-magnitude star, a second-magnitude star is brighter than a third-magnitude star, and so on down to twentieth magnitude or fainter. Each magnitude is 2.5 times as bright as the one below it. Thus a first-magnitude star is 2.5 times as bright as a second-magnitude star and 6.25 times as bright as a third-magnitude star.

After the magnitude scale had been set up, astronomers found that there were some stars even brighter than first magnitude. Rather than rework the whole scale, and give new magnitudes to the hundreds of stars they had catalogued already, they gave these extra-bright stars fractional magnitudes such as 0.8 or 0.1, and to the very brightest they gave zero or even negative magnitudes. Betelgeuse, for example, has a magnitude of 0.1, while Sirius is rated at −1.4. By way of comparison, the full moon has a magnitude of −12.6, while the sun beams down on us with a rating of −26.7.

The color of a star depends on its temperature. The hottest stars, which range from 45,000° to 90,000° Fahrenheit (25,000° to 50,000° Centigrade) are blue and give off much of their energy in invisible ultraviolet rays. Medium-hot stars, like our own sun, are yellow and average around 10,000° F (5,555° C) at the surface. Cool-burning stars are red and range from 6,000° F

11

(3,333° C) down to 3,000° F (1,666° C). Below this temperature they do not give off visible light.

The temperature at which a star burns depends on its mass, that is, on the amount of matter it contains. Just as a fire of coal or oil produces more heat the larger it is, so do the nuclear reactions in the core of a star. The more fuel, the hotter the fire. A star the size of our sun is automatically limited in its temperature. The cooler, red stars are the lightweights of the universe. The hot stars are the giants. By a kind of stellar justice, the big, hot stars have the shortest lifetimes, while the small, cool stars, burning at a slower rate, last for billions of years longer.

Some of the smallest stars are the densest. The white dwarfs, which have collapsed upon themselves, are so dense that a teaspoonful of matter from one would weigh several tons. There is one white dwarf that is half the size of earth, but one cubic inch of its material would weigh 620 tons (562 metric tons), by astronomers' best estimates.

Many of the stars that look like single stars to the naked eye or even to a telescope are actually multiple. Two or more stars revolve around a common center of gravity, linked to each other by mutual attraction. Very often one of these stars is a giant, while its companion is a dwarf.

The stars, although they look fixed in position to us, are actually moving at tremendous speeds. Some are approaching earth, while others are moving away. Most of the stars that form our familiar constellations are moving in different directions, so that in a few thousand years those constellations may look quite different. But there are some groups of stars that appear to be moving in the same direction at about the same speed. The Pleiades are one such group.

A group of stars that seem to travel together is called a star cluster. Clusters may contain hundreds or thousands of stars, most of them invisible to the naked eye.

Stars have always had somewhat of a magical quality for earthbound man. Even today we speak of a *star* performer. Teachers give *gold stars* to good students. Flags of the United States and many other nations feature stars. A person who gets a bad knock on the head is *seeing stars* (at least, that is how the comic strips show it). And a person wrapped up in some idealistic cause or deeply in love is *starry-eyed.* And when we have a narrow escape, we *thank our lucky stars.*

Astronomers have catalogued well over half a million stars, and the list is steadily growing. Eighty-eight internationally recognized constellations can be seen in the skies. With this wealth of heavenly bodies, it is hard to choose which ones to write about. We have chosen to include the sun, moon, and planets of our own solar system, plus some of the brightest individual stars and a few stars of special interest. Of the constellations, the traditional ones of the zodiac are here, plus such familiar ones as Cassiopeia and Ursa Major, which were important to our distant ancestors. We hope you will have as much fun reading about these heavenly bodies and their stories as we did digging up the facts and fables.

Aldebaran

Bright, red-gold Aldebaran is one of the wedge-shaped group of stars called the Hyades, which form the head of Taurus the Bull. Aldebaran itself is the Bull's right eye, if you picture the Bull facing you. It is a star that figures in many myths from different parts of the world. The name Aldebaran comes from the Arabs. Ancient Arab sky-watchers noticed that the Hyades rose shortly after another bright group of stars called the Pleiades. They called them *Al-Dhabaran*, "The Follower." Eventually the name was used for only the brightest star in the Hyades.

Scientifically, Aldebaran is a red giant star, like Antares and Arcturus. It gives off about 130 times as much light as the sun, but it is so distant from earth that only a tiny fraction of that light reaches us.

Taurus was the sign that led off the Babylonian zodiac, and, since Aldebaran is the brightest star in Taurus, it was the most important star of all to those master astronomers of 4,000 years ago. To the ancient Hindus, the same star was a beautiful girl, Rohini, who often wore the shape of a red deer. Rohini was so lovely that her husband, Soma the Moon God, spent all his time with her and neglected his twenty-seven other star-wives. The neglected wives complained to their father, a very influential god. He punished Soma with a staggering curse, which is why the moon goes faint and dark each month.

The Arabs thought of the Hyades as a herd of camels, and they sometimes called Aldebaran the Stallion Camel, the Fat Camel, and, shifting genders, the Female Camel.

In another Arab tale, Aldebaran was a young star-being who courted the stars of the Pleiades. They turned him down because he was poor. So he worked hard and piled up a great fortune, and came back driving the camels of the Hyades ahead of him to show how rich he was. The haughty Pleiades still turned their noses up at him. But Aldebaran must have believed that persistence pays off, for he comes back night after night, still parading his twinkling herd of camels in a vain attempt to impress the girls of his choice.

Algol

Algol comes from the Arabic *al-Ghul,* meaning "The Demon" or "The Ghoul." Its full Arabic name was *Ras-al-Ghul,* "The Demon's Head." In Arab folklore, the ghoul is a particularly horrifying kind of demon that skulks about at night, digging up graves and devouring the corpses. Betweentimes, it lurks in tombs and preys on unwary travelers who are out after dark. With a name like this, it is easy to see that the ancient Arabs regarded Algol as an evil star.

The Arabs were not alone in this belief. The ancient Jews called Algol "Satan's Head" or "Lilith," after the female demon who was Adam's first wife. The Chinese called it "The Piled-Up Corpses." The star seems to have gotten its evil reputation because it appears to blink slowly. The superstitious skywatchers of the ancient world were sure that the blinking star must be the eye of some powerful, extremely evil being glaring down on them, scanning the earth in the hope of finding some chance to do harm.

But the secret of the blinking star has nothing to do with demoniac powers. Actually, Algol is a double star—a pair of stars revolving around each other in orbit. They are so far away from earth that they look like one star to the naked eye, but a good telescope can pick them out easily. When the two stars are side by side, they shine very brightly; when one passes in front of the other it blocks out its partner's light, and the star appears to go dim. The stars pass in front of each other every two and three-fourths days, and the dimming effect lasts about four hours—a short enough time to suggest the slow, menacing wink of a gigantic demon.

Algol is in the constellation Perseus, and its astronomical designation is Beta Persei. Ancient Greek astronomers, seeing that it lay to one side of the main body of the constellation, decided that it must be part of the Gorgon's head that Perseus was holding in his hand. The Gorgons were three beautiful sisters who were turned into monsters by the jealous Hera, chief of the goddesses. They had snakes for hair, and they were so frightful to look at that the mere sight of them turned any living creature to stone. (The ancient Greeks had powerful imaginations!)

Altair

Altair's name comes from an Arabic phrase that means "the Flying Eagle." And Altair itself is the brightest star in the constellation Aquila, "The Eagle." In fact, the brilliant white star is one of the twenty-five brightest visible in the sky. It gives off ten times as much light as the sun. Altair is one of the closer stars to earth, yet it is so far away that its light takes sixteen years to reach us.

The Chinese called Altair the Weaving Star, for they believed it was the Goddess of Weaving. This goddess was a young, beautiful girl, the daughter of the Sun-King who ruled heaven. She fell in love with the young god who took care of the Sun-King's oxen. They were married and lived happily—but not forever after. They spent so much time with each other that they neglected their heavenly jobs. The Sun-King grew quite annoyed as the young lovers disregarded warning after warning. Finally he lost his temper and punished his neglectful daughter and son-in-law by separating them. He placed the Weaving Goddess on one side of the Milky Way and the Herdsman (the star Vega) on the other. The Milky Way in Chinese mythology is a mighty river, so wide and so fierce that not even a god can cross it. So the lovers are separated forever. Except that once a year all the magpies in the world fly up to heaven and hover over the Milky Way, forming a bridge with their wings so that the young goddess can cross over and visit her husband. This is probably the only kind deed the mischievous, noisy magpie has ever been credited with.

Andromeda

Andromeda and its neighboring constellations, Cassiopeia and Cepheus, have enough stories about them to make a novel. To make it brief, Andromeda was the beautiful daughter of Cepheus and Cassiopeia, the King and Queen of Ethiopia. (Some say they were the rulers of the rich seaport city of Joppa, in Phoenicia.) Cassiopeia was a very beautiful woman herself, and together she and her daughter made a stunning pair. Unfortunately, Cassiopeia was also very vain, and she unwisely boasted that she and Andromeda were more beautiful than the Sea-Nymphs, or Nereids.

The Nereids heard of this and flew into a sulk. They ran to their protector, the Sea-God Poseidon, and whined that they had been insulted. The Sea-God decided that he really must put these uppity mortals in their place. So he created a hideous sea-monster named Cetus and sent it off with orders to devastate Ethiopia. *Cetos* is the Greek word for "whale," but this Cetus was not at all like a whale. It was a long, snaky creature with a vicious-looking head and tusks like a wild boar.

Programmed for destruction, Cetus swam off for the coast of Ethiopia, snorting with bestial glee. It paddled along the rocky shore, darting its long, snakelike neck many feet inland and snatching people in its sharp-toothed jaws. Many of the people of Ethiopia were devoured by Cetus. The rest hid in their houses and refused to come out.

Cepheus ordered his soldiers to shoot the beast full of arrows. But the sharp, iron-headed arrows only glanced off the monster's tough scales. In despair, Cepheus went to an oracle and was told that the only way to get rid of the monster was to placate Poseidon by sacrificing Andromeda. So Cepheus had Andromeda chained to a rock at the water line and stood back sadly to await her fate.

Just then the hero Perseus appeared, flying through the air with his winged sandals. Seeing the beautiful girl chained to the rock with a crowd of weeping people standing a safe distance away, he swooped down to ask what the trouble was. Andromeda quickly told him her story. No sooner had she finished than the monster was seen in the distance, making playful leaps out of the water in anticipation of its next meal. Perseus asked Cepheus and Cassiopeia if they would give him Andromeda for his wife if he killed Cetus. They said yes, edging back nervously from the approaching monster.

Perseus soared up in the air, circled over the monster, and swooped down and beheaded it with his magic sickle. Cepheus and Cassiopeia tried to wriggle out of their promise to give their daughter to Perseus, but Andromeda, who had fallen in love with her handsome young rescuer, insisted on going through with the wedding. On their deaths, all of them were placed among the stars to reenact their story. The proud

Cassiopeia was punished by being tied in a chair in a rather uncomfortable position—some say she was really bundled into a market basket like a fat hen. As her stars circle round the North Star, she suffers the extra humiliation of dangling upside down.

The Greeks did not originate this myth of Andromeda and the sea monster. They probably borrowed it from a much older Chaldean myth about Marduk, the Sun-God, and how he killed a sea monster named Tiamat. In the Chaldean myth, the pretty girl was the goddess Ishtar. But Marduk did not rescue her, for she was the one who had created the monster. Instead, he chained her up to prevent her from stirring up more mischief.

In the sky, Andromeda looks like a long, slender V. Its main feature is a famous nebula which modern astronomers have found to be a distant spiral galaxy—a sort of astral cousin to our own Milky Way galaxy.

Cassiopeia is an easily recognized constellation. It looks like a stretched-out W, or an M, depending on which way you are looking at it. It lies opposite from the Big Dipper across the Pole Star, and just about the same distance away. Cassiopeia has no spectacularly bright stars.

Cepheus looks like a badly drawn outline of a house done by a six-year-old artist. It is a rather inconspicuous constellation. But it has three stars that will be Pole Stars in A.D. 4500, 6000, and 7500 respectively. Cepheus has an unusual garnet-colored star that can be seen with the naked eye. It also has a famous variable star.

Antares

Antares' name comes from the Greek *anti*, "against," and *Ares*, the Greek name for Mars, the God of War. Glowing a bright and baleful red in the heart of the Scorpion, it seemed indeed like a rival to Mars, which is what its name really means. To the ancients, both Mars and Antares were stars of evil influence, bringing war, fire, and calamity. In Central Asia, Antares was called "the Gravedigger of Caravans," for superstitious travelers were convinced that if they saw it rising in the morning, robbers and murderers would dog their trail. The Chinese called Antares the Fire Star, from its red color, but they also believed that it could spell success or failure in raising silkworms.

To modern astronomers, Antares has no evil influences, but it is nonetheless a very interesting star. It is the sixteenth brightest star visible from earth, giving out 5,000 times as much light as the sun. It is so bright that it is rated as greater than first magnitude. And it is a supergiant in size, 400 million miles (644 million kilometers) in diameter. Two of earth's orbits could fit inside Antares with plenty of room to spare. The red supergiant has a small, rather dim green companion star, so that Antares is really a double star. However, the green companion cannot be seen without a good telescope.

But, for all its size, Antares is a lightweight. Some astronomers believe its density is so low that it is almost a vacuum. This is typical of the red giant stars, and especially so for those of supergiant size.

Stars become red giants when they have burned up most of their nuclear energy in a last extravagant flareup. They balloon in size. At the same time they cool down, so that they give off red light instead of white (the hottest stars are blue or white). Unusually large stars become supergiants.

The next stage in the red giant's death turns it into a white dwarf, a shrunken, incredibly dense mass that gives off little light or heat. Eventually the white dwarf, its energy all used up, goes cold and dark. But one theory holds that a red supergiant has an even stranger fate. Because of its size, once it begins to shrink it collapses in on itself at a faster and faster rate. Its gravitational attraction becomes so powerful that the star's matter is squeezed into virtually no space at all. Even light rays are trapped by its powerful gravity and cannot escape. The once-brilliant star has become a "black hole" in space.

Aquarius

Aquarius is the Latin word for "water carrier," and the Water Carrier was a very important constellation in the ancient world. From very early times it has been pictured as a man pouring water from a jar or bucket, for it used to be an emblem of the rainy season. The sun's appearance in Aquarius once coincided with the onset of the winter rains in the Middle East and the Mediterranean area, where our astronomy began.

In most cities of the ancient world there was no decent public water supply. Wells and streams were almost always dirty and polluted. So people bought their drinking water from a water carrier who traveled from door to door, like an ice-cream peddler today. The water carrier sold reasonably pure water from a spring or stream far outside the city; he fetched it in big clay jars or in sacks made of animal skins, lashed to a donkey's back. Though most people looked down on the water-carrier, they could not have gotten along without him.

For many centuries Aquarius marked the winter solstice, when the sun was at its weakest, and the powers of cold and darkness seemed to be at their strongest. For ancient peoples it was a time of dread, and they were always glad to see the days grow longer and the sun become warmer once again. For the Chaldeans, Aquarius was a constellation to fear. They lived in the valley of the Euphrates River, where a heavy rain meant a damaging flood. In fact, the Chaldeans were the first people to picture Aquarius as a man pouring out water, which tells us a good deal about how they felt about this constellation.

The Egyptians had a different problem. They almost never got rain, and they depended on the yearly flooding of the Nile to water their fields. They thought of Aquarius as a kindly god who kept the Nile filled from his water jar. Another dry-land people, the Arabs, were so glad to get Aquarius' rain that they gave his stars names such as "The Luckiest of the Lucky."

Aquarius has no bright stars, but it is one of the twelve constellations of the zodiac. In astrology, it is ruled by the planet Uranus; its lucky gem is the garnet, its lucky day is Wednesday, the lucky numbers are 8 and 4, and the lucky colors are pastel blues and greens. Aquarians are supposed to be intelligent, observant, and concerned for the welfare of others.

The earth is now supposed to be moving into the Age of Aquarius, a period of universal love and goodwill. So far the world has had race riots, wars and civil wars, and a wave of crime and terrorism. The astrologers seem pretty far off the beam on this prediction.

Arcturus

Low in the northern sky the ancient Greeks noticed a bright orange star that seemed to follow the Great Bear in its track around the sky, always keeping the same distance from the great star-beast. They named it "The Bear-Guard," which in Greek is *Arcturus*, from *arktos*, "bear," plus *ouros*, "guardian."

Many other peoples besides the Greeks noticed how this bright star seemed to follow the stars of the Great Bear, or Big Dipper, as we call it today. When they thought that this constellation was something other than a bear, they gave Arcturus a suitable role in the stories they made up about the stars. When the Bear was a herd of cattle grazing, Arcturus was the herdsman. When it was a plow, Arcturus was the plowman. When it was a wild beast, Arcturus was a hunter on its trail. Sometimes Arcturus was a sentry, patrolling the border between the southern and the northern stars and seeing to it that each star stayed where it was supposed to be, instead of wandering about and disturbing the order of the heavens.

The fourth brightest star in the northern sky, Arcturus gives off about one hundred times as much light as the sun. Although its color is orange, it is classed as a red giant, superbright, puffed up, and cool. The Hindus were so impressed by Arcturus that they counted it as a sign of the zodiac all by itself, calling it "The Outcast" because it is so far from any other bright stars.

To us, Arcturus is the brightest star in the constellation Boötes, which is a neighbor of Ursa Major. Boötes comes from the Greek for "ox-driver." The Greeks said that Boötes was a son of Demeter, the Earth Goddess, and that his brother had stolen his inheritance. To support himself, Boötes became a farmer and invented the plow to make his work a little easier. (Before the plow was invented, farmers had to dig up the ground with crude, dull spades or pointed sticks before they could plant anything.) In recognition of this great service to mankind, the gods placed Bootes in the sky, while his oxen and plow became Ursa Major (the Great Bear).

The Chinese believed that Arcturus was one of the two horns of the Celestial Dragon who brought in the spring each year, driving out the Tortoise who ruled the winter. (The other horn was Spica, a star that Westerners place in the constellation Virgo, which shows how arbitrary the constellations are.) When the full moon first appeared above the Dragon's horns, it was the signal to China's farmers that spring had truly arrived. It also marked the start of the Chinese New Year. This is why a large figure of a dragon is the central figure of a Chinese New Year's procession. Men inside the dragon, which is made of paper, dance along the street, while a man runs ahead of them holding high a big white ball that represents the moon.

To the Chinese, Arcturus was the most important single star, and Chinese astronomers believed that it ruled the heavens. But Arcturus also had some practical, down-to-earth uses. By its shifting position in the sky it signaled the start of the planting season, the harvest, and other important farm tasks. In the West, too, Arcturus was an important calendar star. Roman farmers knew it was time to harvest their grapes when Arcturus rose in the morning; when it rose in the evening, it meant that the grapevines should get their annual pruning.

Science-fiction writers used to concoct chilling stories about alien monsters from the (imaginary) planets orbiting Arcturus. These BEMs (sci-fi slang for Bug-Eyed Monsters) came in their technologically advanced space ships to conquer and ravage the earth, but were always defeated (whew!) at the last moment. However, until space travel between the stars becomes a reality, we shall never knew whether or not Arcturus has planets, let alone intelligent beings able to build space ships. For, even traveling at the speed of light, it would take thirty-two years to reach Arcturus.

Aries

Aries, the Ram, is one of the faintest constellations in the sky, but to people of ancient times it was one of the most important. For over 2,000 years—from 2000 B.C. to A.D. 100— it was Aries that brought in the spring. The sun rose in Aries when the spring equinox came and the days began to get longer than the nights; to the people of those long-gone times it was a sure sign that spring had really come.

Not knowing that the seasons of the year followed a natural pattern, the ancients believed that spring had to be created each year by the will of the gods. If the gods were unfavorable—and you never could tell—winter would last on and on. In beliefs like this the people were encouraged by their priests, who made a very nice living off the fees people paid them to persuade the gods to be nice.

So, when the stars of Aries hung low on the horizon just before dawn, and the sun rose among them, men and women knew that the cold, dark winter had been defeated for another year, and that they could go ahead and plow their fields and plant their crops.

Aries is the Latin word for "ram," a male sheep. The ram is a very old symbol of male fertility and vigor, and sheep are the first of man's domestic animals to bring forth their young in the spring. Probably lambing time in the ancient Near East and Mediterranean worlds came at the time of the spring equinox. So rams—and lambs—have been traditional spring symbols since man first began to write down his history and probably long before then. The idea that Aries is a ram goes back long before the Romans, who were Johnny-come-latelies in the ancient world, with their history only going back to 750 B.C. It probably began with the Babylonians, who flourished around 2000 B.C., when the spring sun first moved into Aries.

Around 6000 B.C. Aries marked the winter solstice, when the shortest day of the year is reached and the days gradually begin to grow longer. For people in the Middle East back then, this was the most important happening of the year. Only when they learned to farm, instead of living off wild plants and whatever animals they could catch, did spring become more important. Something of Aries' old importance may have lingered on in half-remembered traditions handed down from father to son, to be revived when Aries became the sign of spring.

Today it is Pisces and not Aries that is the spring constellation, and in three or four thousand years Aries will have moved around to the position of the summer solstice, the longest day of the year. These "moves" of the constellations occur because the earth's axis is not steady. It wobbles in a circle like a top that is running down, only much, much more slowly. As earth's axis makes its circle through space, the constellations appear to alter their positions in the frame of the sky, though really it is earth's frame that is shifting. The phenomenon is called the

Precession of the Equinoxes. It takes about 25,800 years for earth to work its way completely around the circle, and about 2,100 years for each shift of the constellations.

There are several myths about how Aries became a constellation. One tells of a war between the Greek gods and the Titans. The Titans were giant cousins of the gods who dwelled on Mount Olympus. They were also the gods' bitter rivals. One day during a lull in the fighting between gods and Titans, the gods went down to Egypt for a picnic and a swim in the Nile. As they were splashing about in the water or frolicking on the banks of the river, the dreaded Typhon crept up on them. Typhon was the largest monster ever born. He had the head of a wild ass, and his legs were coiled serpents. His hideously long arms ended in bunches of serpents' heads instead of hands. When he stood up straight, his head touched the stars, and his filthy wings blotted out the sun. When he opened his mouth, flaming rocks shot out.

When the gods saw Typhon, they panicked and fled. Some turned into animals to disguise themselves; others jumped into the river to hide. Great Zeus turned himself into a ram and ambled off sheepishly, pretending to look for grass somewhere else. In memory of his narrow escape, he placed a ram among the stars.

Another legend tells of Phrixus and Helle, the children of a petty Greek king named Athamas. The two children were about to be sacrificed to atone for some sin of their father's when the god Hermes took pity on them and sent a magical ram with wings and a golden fleece to rescue them. Just in the nick of time, the children jumped on the ram's back and flew off to safety, clinging to his golden wool. Only one of them survived the trip, however. Helle unwisely looked down, became dizzy, lost her grip, and fell to her death in the sea. Phrixus arrived safely in a distant kingdom named Colchis, sacrificed the ram in thanks to Zeus, and hung its fleece up in a temple, where it was guarded by a dragon. Zeus placed the ram's spirit in the sky as a reward for faithful service.

The Greek astronomer Hipparchus, who lived in the second century B.C., made up a calendar of the many yearly changes in the stars. He began the New Year with the spring equinox, when the Sun entered Aries. Astronomers still use the "first point of Aries" as the starting point for the astronomical year, even though Aries has not been the constellation of spring for nearly 2,000 years. And in astrology Aries still leads off the yearly parade of the zodiac.

To astrologers, Aries rules the head and brains. Its gems are amethyst and diamond (every constellation of the zodiac had its special gems, which ancient peoples believed had magical powers). Its colors are bright shades of red. Aries' lucky day is Tuesday, and its lucky numbers are six and seven. Astrology books have pages and pages to say about Aries people (as they do about those born under every sign). The main points are that Aries people are active, dynamic, intelligent, and impulsive, perhaps a bit like a ram butting everything in sight that moves.

Asteroid

Asteroid comes from the Greek *aster*, "star," and the ending *oeides*, which means "having the shape of" or "like." But, though their name means "starlike," asteroids are not stars. They are actually a large swarm of small, planetlike bodies that orbit the sun. Most of them lie in the space between Mars and Jupiter.

The asteroids are much smaller than even the smallest planet, Mercury. The largest asteroid, known as Ceres, is only about 480 miles (773 kilometers) in diameter, while Mercury is about 3,025 (4,880 kilometers). The smallest asteroids are a mile or two across—mere specks of rock compared to the planets. Anything smaller is classed as a meteorite. Only one asteroid, Vesta, reflects enough light to be seen (now and then) with the naked eye. The rest of the larger asteroids are barely visible even with a powerful telescope.

Because of their small size and invisibility, man did not even suspect the asteroids' existence until the late 1700s, when a German astronomer named Johann Bode found that the planets lay at regular distances from the sun, according to a mathematical pattern. Between Mars and Jupiter there lies a mysterious gap where a planet, according to his calculations, ought to be. While searching for this "missing planet," an Italian astronomer named Giuseppe Piazzi discovered the asteroid Ceres in 1801. **1935388**

Within the next few years three more big asteroids were discovered and named Pallas, Juno, and Vesta (for various Greek and Latin goddesses). Most of the other asteroids were not discovered until after 1845, when astronomers first attached cameras to their telescopes. On a long-exposure film, an asteroid shows up as a streak of light because it moves against the background of stars.

Since the 1890s, about 2,000 asteroids have been discovered, and there may be many more. Their origin has never been explained in a way that satisfies all astronomers, but they may have been created by the disintegration of a planet that once spun in an orbit between Mars and Jupiter. Another theory holds that they were formed from a cloud of cosmic dust that never quite pulled together enough to form a full-sized planet.

Science-fiction writers often use asteroids in their stories as transfer stations or refueling stops for interplanetary rockets. Someday they may actually be used for this, although they are too far from earth to make really convenient space platforms. And they don't have enough gravity to hold an atmosphere, so any space travelers from earth would have to carry their own breathing supply with them. But if space travel does become a regular thing, it would not be impossible to fit some of the smaller asteroids with rocket propulsion and dwelling chambers and bring them into a more convenient orbit where they could be used as space stations.

Astrology

Astrology comes from the Greek words *aster*, "star," and *logos*, "word." Literally, it means "words about the stars." And millions of words have been written and spoken about the supposed influence of the stars and planets on human nature and human fate, which is what astrology is all about. People who believe in astrology claim that the positions of the sun, moon, stars, and planets at the moment of your birth decide the sort of character you will have, and their changing positions from day to day influence what is going to happen to you that day. Of course, there is no scientific proof that astrologers' predictions come true, but some people like to believe in it anyway.

Scientists consider astrology nothing but superstition. Astrologers insist that it is a science. It could be described as an application of scientific methods to thoroughly unscientific ideas. But if astrology is a wayward child of astronomy, it is also its ancestor.

The idea that the stars had power probably began far back in prehistoric times, when primitive man noticed that some stars appeared at certain positions in the sky at different times of the year. Once he had matched the stars with the changing of the seasons, it was not unreasonable for him to think that the stars controlled the seasons. Therefore the stars must be gods, and gods can control the destinies of people as well as the seasons.

Astrology and astronomy as we know them began with the Sumerians, who lived in the Middle East (in the region that is now Iraq) about 4000 B.C. Sumerian astronomers mapped out the zodiac and its constellations. (Their constellations were somewhat different from ours since they visualized them differently.) They plotted the paths of the stars and planets and worked out elaborate mathematical calculations to predict their motions and when each one would reappear at a certain point in the sky. The Babylonians, who came along after the Sumerians, took over their ideas and improved upon them. So far, astronomy and astrology were the same thing. Insofar as scientific astronomy existed, it was to help the priests make better observations of the stars so they could make more accurate predictions.

Babylonian ideas about astrology reached Greece about the middle of the fourth century B.C. They reached Rome before the beginning of the Christian Era. They also spread to India and eventually to China, where they mingled with the native ideas. Astrology was extremely popular in the Roman Empire, and astrologers did a flourishing business. They were usually knowns as "Chaldeans" or mathematicians. The Chaldeans were a people who took over the empire of Babylon, and many writers about astronomy use the names interchangeably. The Babylonians and Chaldeans had the greatest reputations in astrology in the ancient world, so astrologers claimed to be Chaldean just the way that a restaurant cook today might claim to be French, cashing in on the national reputation.

But it was the Greeks who invented modern astrology, taking it far beyond the point the Babylonians had reached. They devised a fantastically complicated system based on the positions of the heavenly bodies at the moment of a person's birth—in fact, they devised a number of competing systems. Each planet was assigned qualities of character—for instance, Jupiter stood for justice and virtue, while Mars stood for a quarrelsome nature. The astrologers also decided that each planet ruled one or more of the constellations of the zodiac and the days of the week.

They didn't stop there. Each planet and each sign of the zodiac was assigned its own colors, gemstones, metals, healing and poisonous herbs, animals, and parts of the human body. This last bit of pseudoscience was arrived at by a diagram called the Grand Man. Astrologers laid out the circle of the zodiac and drew a man bent backward around it, so that his head rested on the soles of his feet. The head was placed in Aries, the first sign of the zodiac. The feet belonged in Pisces, the last sign. All the other parts of the body were ruled by whatever sign they fell into on this diagram. Many doctors would not treat an illness if the astrological signs that ruled the ailing part of the body were not in the right position. Considering the kind of medicine they practiced, perhaps the patient was better off not being treated.

The Greeks also invented the horoscope—the day-to-day prediction of one's fortune. When you read your horoscope in the daily paper or a magazine, you have the ingenious speculation of some old-time Greek to thank.

Astrology continued as a powerful influence at least down to the early 1600s. Rulers had astrologers on their staffs and consulted them before making any important decision, just as a modern business executive may seek the advice of a management consultant. In fact, some of the great pioneers of modern astronomy, such as Tycho Brahe, Gassendi, and Kepler, began as astrologers. But their discoveries started a chain reaction in science that in time made educated people stop taking astrology seriously.

Astrology is still very much with us today, however. Books and magazines on astrology are sold at almost every newstand. Daily papers carry horoscope columns. Astrologers appear as guests on TV talk shows. Many amateur astrologers get great enjoyment from casting their friends' horoscopes. Even some heads of nations believe in astrology. Hitler, the evil dictator of Germany from 1933 to 1945, was a strong believer in astrology and had an astrologer on his personal staff. And in 1975 the President of Argentina, Isabel Perón, had an astrologer as her chief cabinet minister. Since this man was also head of the secret police, he was in an excellent position to make his predictions about Argentinians come true.

Today's astrologers have two specialties: character analysis and horoscopes. They have painstakingly worked-out calculations and tables that tell them where the important heavenly bodies were at your birth, where they will be tomorrow, and where they will be the day you have to take a big math test, have a job interview, and so on. Some astrologers even use computers. For several years in the 1960s a large computerized astrologer's booth stood in Grand Central Station, in New York City. For five dollars you could get a character reading; for seven fifty you could also get your horoscope for the next twelve months.

For many people today, astrology serves a purpose even though they don't believe in it wholeheartedly. For some, it is a handy cop-out: "I can't help losing my temper all the time. Look, I was born under a bad aspect of Aries!" For others, it is something to make conversation about, or to start flirtations with. For many people, it is a harmless amusement. In any case, it will have its followers as long as people like to believe in strange powers beyond our control.

Astronomy

Astronomy is the scientific study of the stars and other heavenly bodies. It takes in everything from the amateur star-watcher with a pair of binoculars to the highly trained scientist analyzing radio waves given off by distant stars or calculating the nuclear reactions in their hearts. The word *astronomy* is Greek and means "distribution of the stars."

The earliest known astronomers were the Sumerians, who lived in the Middle East. (See the entry on ASTROLOGY.) This part of the world was a natural spot for man to watch the skies, for its air is usually dry and clear. Through trade and conquest, the Sumerians' ideas spread to other peoples and eventually reached large parts of Europe, Asia, and North Africa. The Chinese developed their own astronomy, which set the pattern for eastern Asia, although some Middle Eastern ideas also reached them. The great Indian civilizations of Mexico, Central America, and South America also developed their own astronomies. At the time the Spaniards conquered them, in the fifteen hundreds, the Indians were better astronomers than the Europeans, for they had a better mathematical system that enabled them to make more accurate calculations.

Old-time astronomy was closely tied to religion and superstition, for it was a part of astrology. A few Greek philosophers before the Christian Era had tried to point out that the stars and planets were natural bodies, not gods, but no one paid attention to them. A Christian bishop in Spain, Isidore of Seville, around A.D. 600 also suggested that the heavenly bodies should be studied for their own sakes as well as to foretell the future. But astronomy did not begin to break away from astrology until the late 1500s, when Copernicus, Tycho Brahe, and Johannes Kepler made discoveries that completely overturned the old ideas about the universe and its makeup. Perhaps the most important of their contributions was proving that earth is not the center of the universe and that earth revolves around the sun, instead of the sun around earth.

Another revolution in astronomy came when the telescope was invented (about 1608, probably by a Dutch lens-grinder named Hans Lippershey). When Galileo down in Italy learned of the marvelous new instrument, he immediately made his own and used it to study the heavens. The discoveries he made in 1609 and 1610 with this crude, one-inch spyglass were nothing short of amazing. The moon, he saw, was filled with mountains and craters, and large, dark areas that he mistook for water (he named them *maria*, Latin for "seas"). The sun's face was marked by dark spots that came and went mysteriously. Venus waxed and waned like the moon. Jupiter had moons of its own. New stars too faint to see with the naked eye suddenly appeared when the telescope was trained on them. Galileo also discovered the rings of Saturn, although he was never sure whether they were real or an optical illusion.

Until the invention of the telescope, astronomy was limited to studying the motions and positions of those stars and planets that could be seen with the naked eye. With the telescope, astronomers could now begin to study the nature of the heavenly bodies. Some stars were found to be double. The great red spot on Jupiter and the moons of Saturn were discovered before 1700, as telescopes improved rapidly. Isaac Newton worked out the laws of gravitation, which govern the orbits of stars and planets among other things.

By the time Newton had accomplished this, he had already made two other valuable contributions to astronomy. One was inventing the reflecting telescope, which is much better for observing stars than the refracting type that Galileo used, which simply magnified distant objects by means of lenses. The stars are so far distant that no matter how much you magnify them, they still show up in your telescope as tiny dots of light. At the same time, the more powerful you make your lenses, the smaller area of sky they take in. But the reflecting telescope catches a fairly large area of the sky in its concave (dished-in) mirror, and an eyepiece lens lets you magnify this image. Then, too, there is the problem of distortion due to invisible defects in the glass of the lenses, which was more serious in Newton's time than it is today. It is easier to make a mirror free of distortion than a lens.

Newton's other great contribution was his experiments with prisms. He found that a prism could split sunlight into bands of different colors, in fact, all the colors of the rainbow. By passing this light through another prism, he could combine the colored rays back into white light. Newton's experiments laid the foundation for the science of *spectroscopy* (literally, "ghost-looking"—some imaginative scientist must have thought Newton's prismatic colors were the "ghost" of the light he had killed by splitting it up). By analyzing the light given off by a star, scientists can now learn which chemical elements are present in the star, and the proportions of each one. Helium was discovered in the sun by this means. Spectroscopy has also revealed many double stars that were too faint or too close together to be detected by a telescope. Light reflected from a planet can also be analyzed by a spectroscope.

The invention of photography in the 1800s gave astronomers another valuable tool. By mounting a camera on a telescope and focusing it on a given area of the sky for a long period, the film could capture details that the eye could not. (Photographic telescopes have motor-driven mounts that keep them pointed at the same spot in the sky despite the earth's turning.) Another advantage was that the photograph could be kept on hand and studied whenever necessary, and that many people could study it. With a telescope, only one person at a time can see. The first astronomical photograph (of the moon) was taken in 1840. Since then, the camera-telescope has made many important discoveries. One of them was the planet Pluto.

Radio astronomy came into being in the early 1930s when a young engineer at Bell Telephone Laboratories, Karl Jansky, was given the job of eliminating static in transoceanic radio telephone communications. To do this, Jansky had to find out where the static came from. So he built a gigantic radio receiver and discovered that there were three kinds of static: bangs from thunderstorms nearby, clicks from faraway thunderstorms, and a strange steady hissing that came from outer space. Jansky published his findings in 1932. Nothing more was done until 1937, when a Chicago radio engineer named Grote Reber read Jansky's work and built his own radio telescope in his backyard, a large, dish-shaped reflector that gathered radio signals and focused them on a receiver. Reber was able to detect radio waves from the Milky Way and map them. Now a number of countries have very large radio telescopes—the largest at present is at Arecibo, in Puerto Rico. It covers nineteen acres of ground.

All stars and nebulas give off radio waves as well as light and heat. The radio waves travel much greater distances than the other forms of radiation. So a radio telescope can pick up waves from stars, galaxies, and nebulas much too distant for a visual telescope, even a photographic one. By analyzing the faint radio signals from space, astronomers can actually map these galaxies that they can hear but cannot see. The most distant galaxy known, discovered in 1975, is about 8 billion light-years distant from the sun. This means that the signals from this galaxy that astronomers pick up today started out 8 *billion years ago!* They may have started off at the time when the universe itself was born.

Since the late 1950s, spacecraft have permitted scientists to observe stars and planets without interference by earth's atmosphere—a tremendous improvement. Manned expeditions to the moon have made valuable discoveries. Even more about our neighbors in the solar system has been learned from unmanned spacecraft that transmit photos and measurements of temperature, magnetism, and similar data back to earth. Flybys of the planets have yielded information that completely changes many of our ideas about them. In years to come, space probes and orbiting observatories will give us still more knowledge and understanding of our universe.

Betelgeuse

Surely one of the oddest of all star names is Betelgeuse, pronounced "beetle-jooz." The name is a French corruption of the star's Arabic name, *Ibt-al-Jauzah* or *Bayt-al-Jauz*. *Ibt-al-Jauzah* literally means "armpit of the central one," but this inelegant name is usually translated into English as "shoulder of the giant." In fact, Betelgeuse *is* the star that marks the right shoulder of the giant Orion, and "the Giant" is one of the most frequently used names for Orion in the Middle East. *Al-Jauzah* originally meant a black sheep with a white spot in the middle of its body. Later it came to stand for anything central, and Orion travels across the center of the sky when viewed from the Arab lands. *Bayt-al-Jauz*, the other name the dictionaries give, has been translated as "House of the Giant" and "House of the Twins." Obviously, some translator was not very sure of his Arabic.

Betelgeuse is a red giant, a type of star that has passed its peak and ballooned in size as it ages, at the same time losing much of its energy. Eventually it will become a white dwarf. But Betelgeuse is still many millions of years away from the pallid, corpselike stage of white dwarfdom. Right now it is a red supergiant, giving off 17,000 times as much light as our own sun and ranging from 300 to 420 times the sun's diameter. Betelgeuse varies in size because it expands and contracts rhythmically as the nuclear fires at its heart flare up and die down.

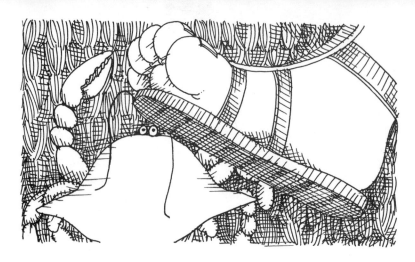

Cancer

Cancer is the faintest of all the constellations in the zodiac. It is almost impossible to see unless the atmosphere is very clear and still. But in ancient times Cancer was quite important because it marked the summer solstice. This is probably why it got its name, which is Latin for "crab," for Cancer marked the point at which the sun stopped advancing northward in the sky and began to sidle back toward the south, like a crab on a beach. To this day we give the name of Tropic of Cancer to the imaginary line on the earth's surface that marks the northernmost point where the sun stands directly overhead at noon. The word *tropic*, by the way, is Greek for "turning point." The regions we call the tropics lie between the sun's northern and southern turning points, the Tropics of Cancer and Capricorn.

Although Cancer contains no stars of more than fourth magnitude, which is pretty faint, it does contain a large star cluster easily visible with binoculars. It is called *Praesepe* (Latin for "manger") or "the Beehive." A pair of stars on opposite sides of the manger are known as the Northern and the Southern Ass, for the Greeks and Arabs thought of them as two asses feeding from the same manger.

Cancer itself was supposedly a crab that Hera sent out of spite to attack Hercules while he was fighting the monstrous Hydra, a water creature with nine wolfish heads. The crab dutifully gave Hercules a vicious nip in the foot, whereupon he stepped hard on the little pest and crushed it. Hera gave the crab the customary consolation prize of a place in the sky, but she couldn't have been very pleased with its work, because she gave it only faint stars.

The Chaldeans believed that Cancer was the gate through which souls left heaven to enter human bodies. The idea was picked up by the Greek philosopher Plato and his followers, who spread it throughout the Mediterranean world, giving Cancer an extra importance in astrology.

Astrologically, Cancer stands for the ability to stick to one's purpose. The lucky day is Monday; the lucky numbers are one and three; and the lucky colors are silver and white—moon colors, for Cancer is ruled by the moon. Cancerians are said to be reflective and sensitive, qualities that hardly apply to a small-brained, hard-shelled crab.

Capella

Capella, the "little she-goat," is the brightest star in the constellation Auriga, the Charioteer. *Capella* is a Latin name, and it comes from *caper*, the word for a male goat, plus the diminutive *ell*, which carries the idea of something small, plus the ending *a*, which shows that the whole thing is feminine. In Greek astro-mythology, Capella represents the she-goat that suckled Zeus when he was being raised in hiding from his murderous father, Cronos.

Auriga is a very strangely named constellation. It looks nothing at all like the charioteer whose Latin name it bears. It is a badly distorted pentagon, and one of its corner stars, the "charioteer's" right foot, really belongs to Taurus as the tip of the Bull's left horn. Nevertheless, the Greeks and Romans chose to see in it the picture of a charioteer with no chariot and no horses. His reins and whip are gathered in his right hand, and on his left shoulder he carries a she-goat. On his left forearm he carries two small kids.

The Greeks claimed that Auriga was Erichthonius, whose name may mean "wool on the earth" or "from the land of heather." Erichthonius was the son of Hephaestos the blacksmith god and Athene. A cripple like his father, he supposedly invented the four-horse chariot so that he could get from place to place. For this useful invention Zeus rewarded him by first making him the king of Athens and then putting his image in lights in the sky. What this crippled inventor-godling has to do with goats is difficult to understand. Probably the Greeks took a much older myth and tailored it to fit their own stories.

The idea of Auriga as a goatherd is several thousand years old. A sculpture found in the ruins of an ancient Middle Eastern city that flourished not long after 1000 B.C. shows Auriga in this form, and the myth must be much older than that. Through most of the Middle East, Capella was thought of as a goatherd's or shepherd's star, and the Greeks and Romans also liked the idea. An old English name for Capella was "the Shepherd's Star."

A name invented by the Romans was "the rainy goat-star," for Capella has long been linked with the onset of the Mediterranean rainy season and with stormy winter winds. Shepherds and farmers welcomed the star for bringing life-giving water to their pastures and fields, which were dry and scorched after the long, rainless Mediterranean summer. Sailors dreaded it because it brought storms.

Capella is the third brightest star visible in the northern sky, and it was important in many ancient religions. The Hindus worshiped it as the sacred Heart of Brahma, the Creator of the Universe. The Egyptians built one or more temples oriented on Capella, which they seem to have identified with the god

Ptah. Ptah began as a local god of artists and craftsmen, but his cult grew so that he ended up as one of the most important gods of ancient Egypt. In an Egyptian version of the zodiac, Capella was shown as a mummified cat held in the hand of a male god who wore a crown of feathers. The cat was a sacred animal in ancient Egypt, ranking almost as high as the baboon.

North of the equator, Capella can be seen on any clear night of the year, but it is best seen in winter, when it is highest in the sky. One of the twenty-five brightest stars, it gives off about 140 times as much light as the sun. Its color has been described variously as yellow, golden, white, red, and blue. Most modern astronomers call it yellow.

Capella is actually a double star, but its two components are too close together for a telescope to distinguish. The fact that it is double was discovered only when Capella's light was analyzed with a spectroscope.

Strangely, the Incas of South America thought of Capella as a herdsman's star, though their herds were llamas and alpacas instead of goats and sheep. It is strange because the Incas' civilization flourished centuries after the downfall of the Roman Empire, in a part of the world cut off from Europe and Asia by wide oceans. They could not have heard of the ancient lore about the Shepherd's Star. Unless, as some people suggest, a shipload of Phoenicians or Egyptians, caught in a storm at sea, somehow drifted to South America and made their way to the high Andes.

Capricorn

Capricorn, or Capricornus, to give it its scientific name, is the tenth constellation of the zodiac. Since the earliest known times it has been pictured as a goat with the tail of a fish—carvings of it have been found on long-buried stone markers in the ruins of Babylon.

The Greeks told a comical myth about the origin of Capricorn. They traced it to the famous swimming party of the gods in Egypt while the gods were at war with their giant kinsmen the Titans. When the monster Typhon made his appearance, Pan, who was half goat, tried to become all goat. But he leaped into the river before the change was complete, so that his rear half turned into fish form. Zeus, disguised as a ram, looked nervously back over his shoulder to see if Typhon was following him. He caught sight of Pan and burst into bleats of laughter. Afterward he placed the image of the goat-fish in the sky as a reminder of Pan's comical appearance.

Scholars believe the Greek myth was an attempt to explain the old Babylonian symbol of the goat-fish. The goat symbol may come from the fact that Capricorn marks the low point of the sun in the sky. After reaching this point—the winter solstice—the sun turns in its path and climbs the sky again. Probably the Babylonians hoped that if they pictured the sun as a goat it would scamper up the sky as a frisky young goat scampers up a hillside. The fish tail almost certainly symbolized the rains and floods of the Middle Eastern winter.

The constellation Capricornus bears no resemblance to either a goat or a fish. It looks like a broad arrowhead or an upside-down cocked hat. It has no first-magnitude stars, but it contains several colorful double stars that can be seen with a telescope.

In astrology, Capricorn represents sin (the goat is a symbol of sin in Jewish, Christian, and Moslem traditions) and also regeneration. It also symbolizes the rebirth of the sun and the coming of mankind's Redeemer. It is ruled by the planet Saturn. The lucky gem is onyx; the lucky day, Saturday; the lucky numbers, seven and three; the lucky color, dark green. Capricorns are said to be charming, serious, and patient, and to get along well with people.

One of the oldest known astrological predictions concerned Capricorn. It is thought to have come from the records of Sargon, a Middle Eastern emperor who ruled about 2800 B.C. His stargazers warned that the world would be destroyed by fire if ever the five planets met in the house of Capricorn. About 350 years later, Chinese astronomers noted that the planets did meet in Capricorn. But they had no disasters to report. After all, it wasn't *their* prediction.

Comet

"When beggars die, there are no comets seen; the heavens themselves blaze forth the death of princes!" cried Shakespeare in his great tragedy *Julius Caesar*. With these dramatic lines, Shakespeare expressed a belief that was taken quite seriously in his time. Indeed, since the earliest civilizations men had looked on comets as supernatural messengers warning of horrible disasters and catastrophes. (And rulers, of course, liked to think of their own deaths as the worst possible kind of catastrophe for their subjects.)

In prescientific days it was easy to imagine that a comet was a sort of brightly burning bad angel, rushing through the sky with its long, flaming hair trailing out far behind it, bringing plagues, earthquakes, and wars. When a comet passed across the heavens, pious folk would pray energetically and make big gifts to temples and churches to ward off divine anger.

The name *comet* comes from the Greek *aster kometes*, "long-haired star." Today, however, we know that comets are simply masses of ice crystals, frozen gases, and cosmic dust. Some astronomers call them "dirty snowballs." But comets are not dense-packed like snowballs. They are more like a thick cloud of windblown snow. The comets that we see have three parts. The densest is the nucleus, which is in the center of the comet's head. Around the nucleus is a thin cloud of gases called the *coma*. From the coma is formed the tail, which may be as much as 100 million miles long.

Current theory holds that there is a belt of comets circling the sun 14 billion miles (22.5 billion kilometers) out in space. Now and then some outside force unbalances a comet and starts it into a new orbit. Some comets whiz once past the sun and back into the outer zone, never to return. Some travel too close to the sun and disintegrate. A few go into a regular orbit and return within view of earth at periodic intervals.

In far outer space, comets are apparently rather small, only a few miles across, with no tail. But as they approach the sun, they are bombarded with solar energy. This heats them, making them swell up and become spongy. Some of their ice crystals and frozen gases melt and break up. The force of the sun's radiation pushes some of this gas and dust into a streaming tail behind the comet's body, as a strong wind can blow a cloud into a new shape. The force of solar radiation is very small, but it is enough to push the thin stuff of a comet about. As comets swing away from the sun, their tails gradually disappear.

Comets travel at a speed of thousands of miles per hour, but their orbits are so long that it may take them hundreds of years to return to a given point. Some thirty comets have periods of 1,000 to 10,000 years. But a few comets have very short periods. The shortest is Encke's comet, which passes earth every thirty months. Another, with the mouth-filling name of Schwassmann-Wachmann II, has a period of six and a half years. (Like all other comets, Schwassmann-Wachmann was named for its discoverers.)

The best-known comet of all is Halley's comet, which returns every seventy-six years. First seen in 476 B.C., it was not recognized as a periodic visitor until A.D. 1682, when an English astronomer named Edmund Halley got the idea that perhaps some comets did return, and worked out its probable orbit. The great American writer Mark Twain was born under Halley's comet in 1835. In 1066, just before the battle in which the Norman invaders defeated the Saxons, a fiery comet (now known to be Halley's) flew over Europe. The famous Bayeux Tapestry, a kind of embroidered medieval action-comic strip, shows terrified townsmen staring and pointing at the dreaded apparition. Apparently the Saxons took it as a bad omen and the Normans as a good omen. But the Norman victory was probably due to the fact that the Saxon army had marched over one hundred miles with little rest after fighting a hard battle in the north of England.

Seventy-five years or so ago, "comet" was a synonym for anything speedy. Crack express trains were sometimes named The Comet. Today's traveler stuck on a delayed train must often suspect he has hitched a ride on a comet with a thousand-year orbit.

Constellation

Constellation is a group of stars that seem to belong together and form fixed patterns or figures in the sky, such as the Big Dipper, Orion, and Cassiopeia. (These are the patterns they form when seen from earth. To someone on another planet, the star patterns would look entirely different because of the difference in viewpoints.) The stars of a constellation are actually millions of miles apart, and they may all be moving in different directions. But they are so far away from earth that it takes thousands of years for their positions to change enough to be noticed by an earth observer.

Most of the constellations' names are very ancient. Some have come down to us from the earliest civilizations in the Middle East, where the study of astronomy began. The constellations, once their shapes were traced out by long-forgotten men, were passed down among Egyptians, Babylonians, Hebrews, Greeks, and Romans, keeping pretty much the same outlines though often changing their names to fit different peoples' myths. The names we use today are Latin names. *Constellation* itself comes from the Latin word *constellatio*, which comes from *cum*, "with" or "together," and *stella*, "star." Roughly speaking, it means "star-togetherness," or "a bunch of stars." But the Romans themselves never talked about a *constellatio*, for the word was apparently not coined until about A.D. 1300, by medieval scholars. The Romans used the words *sidus* or *signum*.

It is really a puzzle how the constellations came by their names, since only a few look the least bit like what they are supposed to represent. There are three possible explanations. One is that long ago the constellations really did look more like lions, bulls, and heavenly queens than they do now. Another is that ancient peoples had much more vivid imaginations than we do. The third, and probably the most likely, is that ancient peoples simply named the constellations after gods and heroes and magical animals that were important in their own mythology, just as today we name streets and airports and mountains after important people.

For example, Aries the Ram doesn't look at all like a ram, or indeed like any recognizable figure. But about 4,000 years ago it was Aries that announced the coming of spring. The ram was an ancient symbol of springtime, and this is probably why its name was given to the stars that brought in the spring.

Aries is one of the constellations of the zodiac, a system of twelve constellations devised by ancient Middle Eastern astronomers to keep track of the movement of the sun and the changing of the seasons. Most of the other constellations are named for characters from Greco-Roman mythology. But not all—in the late seventeenth century, European astronomers decided to modernize the map of the sky and split up some of the old constellations, giving the leftover pieces new names. In honor of science, they named some of the new constellations after scientific instruments. This is why we have constellations with names like Telescopium and Microscopium.

The ancient peoples of the Mediterranean and the Near East generally agreed on the shapes of the constellations, for they had so much contact with each other. In other parts of the world, men put the stars together in quite different patterns. To ancient Chinese astronomers, for instance, part of the constellation Sagittarius formed the Tiger, while the rest of it was joined with Scorpio, Libra, and part of Virgo to form the Azure Dragon.

The biggest difference came in the names. Each group of people attached a different meaning to the constellations. Our Big Dipper, for instance, was a Great Bear to Greeks, Romans, and Iroquois Indians. But to the Arabs, it was a huge Coffin holding a slain hero, with a procession of mourners following after it. To the Chinese, it was a Grain Measure.

Constellations were originally important because they were man's first calendars. Primitive man had no system of writing, and no way of keeping track of time other than by cutting notches in a stick for each day. But he had learned that certain groups of stars appeared on the horizon at sunrise or sunset at definite times of the year. Hunters, herdsmen, and farmers could watch the constellations and tell when the rainy season, the dry season, the cold season, and the warm season were due. Since primitive men tended to believe that the orderly progress of the seasons depended on the good will of the gods, they were always relieved to see the constellations appear when they were supposed to. This meant that for another season everything would be all right.

Later—but still in ancient times—men began to make long sailing voyages on the sea, out of sight of land. They used the constellations as their guides in navigating. The Polynesians, who settled on many of the scattered islands of the Pacific, were masters of the art of navigating by the stars, for they had no compasses to tell them their direction. Chinese, Hindus, Arabs, Phoenicians, and Europeans also used the stars as guides. And even in this day of radio beacons, navigating by the stars is still a useful skill. So the constellations are still important to man. Even without this practical use, they would still be important to scientists and star-watchers to bring some order into the thousands of visible stars in the sky.

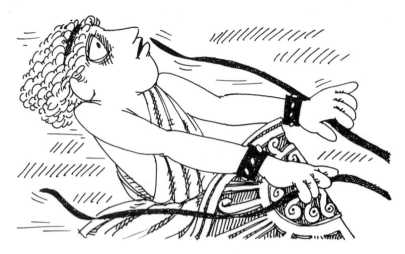

Deneb

Deneb, or Dhanab, is the Arabic word for "tail"—and it appears in the names of several stars, such as *Deneb Kaitos*, "Tail of the Whale," *Denebola*, "Lion's Tail," and *Deneb-al-Gedi*, "Tail of the Goat." But one star is known simply as Deneb. It marks the "tail" of the constellation Cygnus. This constellation has appeared in different guises to different peoples, but almost always as some kind of bird. To the Arabs, it was a noble, soaring eagle. To some later peoples, it was a hen. The Chinese thought of it as a magpie. In Christian times, it has been called the Northern Cross. But to the Greeks it was a swan, flying with its long neck outstretched.

Brilliant white Deneb is not only the brightest star in Cygnus; it is one of the brightest that can be seen from earth. Astronomers believe that it is probably the brightest of all, with a light output about 10,000 times greater than that of the sun. However, it is so far away (about 1,630 light-years) that it shows up as only the nineteenth brightest to a sky-watcher on earth.

One of the Greek star myths tells that Cygnus was the brother of Phaëthon, one of Apollo's many children by a mortal woman. (If one believes the Greek myths, the gods scattered their children like confetti all over the world, just to show where they had been.) One day Apollo rashly promised Phaëthon that he could drive his golden chariot, the sun. The inexperienced Phaëthon could not control Apollo's four fiery horses that pulled the chariot, and he careened crazily across the sky, coming so near the earth that he began to scorch it. To prevent the irresponsible youth from burning up the entire world, Zeus blasted him to bits with a thunderbolt. The charred fragments of Phaëthon's body fell into a river, while Apollo jumped aboard the runaway sun-chariot and brought it under control. Cygnus, heartbroken, dived time after time into the river to recover his brother's body, until he had found every fragment and Phaëthon could have a proper burial. The gods, as usual, looked on with no attempt to help or even comfort poor Cygnus. Some of them even sniggered that he looked like a duck dabbling for food. But later they were ashamed of their behavior, and they rewarded Cygnus by putting him in the sky as a noble swan, outlined in twinkling stars.

Draco

Draco is the Latin word for a snake or dragon, and Draco the Dragon is a very old constellation. With its lozenge-shaped head and long, S-shaped body it really does suggest some kind of snakelike creature in the sky.

The Dragon probably goes back several thousand years to the mythical sea-serpent Tiamat, a creature of Chaldean mythology. The Chaldeans and other early Near Eastern civilizations believed that Tiamat was the very spirit of evil and chaos. Every now and then Tiamat tried to destroy the world with the aid of scorpion-men and other frightful monsters that she created. But finally she was slain by the Sun-God Marduk.

Far to the north, the Norsemen thought that Draco was the star-picture of the dreaded Midgard Serpent. This was an unimaginably huge snake that twined itself around the center of the world, under the sea. It spent most of its time sleeping quietly with its tail in its mouth, but every now and then it stirred in its sleep and caused an earthquake. At the end of the world the Midgard Serpent would wake up and join in the battle of the giants and other evil creatures against the gods. All of them would kill each other, and the world would be destroyed. But from the ruins a new and better world would be created.

The Greeks had several stories about Draco. In one tale it guarded the golden apples of the Hesperides—islands far off in the Western Ocean where no sane Greek would venture—which Hercules had to fetch as one of his twelve labors. Another story is that it was the dragon which a hero named Cadmus slew on orders from Athene. The goddess then told him to extract the dragon's teeth and sow them in the ground. As soon as he had done this, the dragon's teeth sprouted into armed soldiers, unpleasantly ready for a fight. Rattling their swords against their shields, they looked at Cadmus in a way he did not like at all. But Athene told him to toss a stone into the midst of the armed crowd. It struck one of the soldiers, and he immediately attacked the one standing next to him. The soldiers next to them joined the fray, and in no time at all the whole army was fighting each other. Soon only five were left alive, and they were too weary to fight anymore. Cadmus persuaded them to lay down their arms, and they later became his helpers. But ever since then, "sowing dragon's teeth" has meant stirring up trouble and strife.

In still another Greek myth, Draco joined in one of the great battles between the gods of Olympus and the Titans, but picked the losing side. Athene seized the scaly creature and before it could defend itself hurled it high in the sky, where it remained, close to the Pole Star.

Indeed, some 5,500 years ago Draco did contain the Pole Star, which was then the star Thuban, in the dragon's tail.

(*Thuban* is one of the Arabic words for "dragon.") This star was very important to the ancient Egyptians. They also worshiped one of the Dragon's eyes, the star Eltanin.

Draco is not hard to locate in the sky, for its tail is curled halfway around the Little Dipper. It is interesting to astronomers because it contains many double stars.

One of Draco's neighboring constellations is Hercules, which contains a famous glove-shaped star cluster that astronomers believe is five billion years old and contains about 100,000 stars. The Greek myths connect Hercules with more than one dragonlike monster. But, to the ancient Greeks, this constellation simply looked like a kneeling man, not the legendary hero, and they called it the Kneeler. The name of Hercules did not come into general use for this constellation until a few years before Columbus sailed off to discover what he thought was a short cut to India.

Earth

Earth, the third planet from the sun, is our home planet. At the date when this was written, it was the only planet definitely known to harbor life.

The name *earth* (which also means the soil itself) comes from the Anglo-Saxon word *eorthe*. The Latin names for earth were *Terra* (usually used to mean "dry land" or "soil") and *Tellus*. *Tellus* was the name the Romans usually used when they were talking about the planet. It was also the name of an ancient Earth-Goddess. The Greek name for earth was *ge* (pronounced "gay"), which crops up in a whole string of scientific words like geology, geography, geode, geometry, and a good thirty more.

Peoples of ancient times, and primitive peoples who lived not too long ago, had many different ideas about the creation of the earth. Some American Indian tribes, for example, believed the earth was created by a muskrat or a loon that dived to the bottom of the Great Water which covered everything and brought up a gob of mud. The Great Spirit then formed the mud into the world. The Indians did not explain how the Great

Spirit made a muskrat-mouthful of mud stretch far enough to make such a mass of land. Perhaps that sort of question didn't interest them.

The Greeks had at least five or six explanations of how the earth was created. One of them is rather like our own Bible story of the Creation.

Scientists, however, have different ideas. The most generally accepted theory is that earth, the other planets, and the sun were all formed from a gigantic, whirling cloud of gas and dust floating in space near the edge of the Milky Way galaxy. (See the entry on PLANET for the story of how this happened.) Another theory is that the planets were formed from a mass of blazing matter torn from the sun by another star passing close by.

In any case, the planet we now inhabit measures about 7,900 miles (12,719 kilometers) in diameter, which makes it the fifth largest of the planets in the solar system. Actually, earth is a little fatter than this at the equator (7,927 miles), (12,756 kilometers) because the force of its rotation makes it bulge slightly. But the difference is not very much compared to 7,900 miles.

Earth has a fluid core, which is thought to be mostly iron. Iron, in fact, is the most abundant element in our planet, followed by oxygen, silicon, aluminum, calcium, and magnesium. Eighty-six other elements exist naturally on earth, in relatively tiny quantities. There are also a few man-made elements. Most of these have such short lives that they do not exist anywhere outside the labs where they are made.

A few more basic facts about earth: the highest mountain, Everest, rises about 29,000 feet (8,800 meters) above sea level; the deepest known abyss in the sea floor lies about 36,000 feet (11,000 meters) down in the western Pacific Ocean. The average distance of earth from the sun is about 93,000,000 miles (149,600,000 kilometers), and the time it takes earth to complete one orbit around the sun is what we call one year. As earth circles the sun, it rotates from west to east on its own axis, and one day is what we call the time it takes to make one complete rotation.

Earth's axis is tilted 23.5 degrees away from the plane of its orbit. Because of this tilt, each part of the planet gets a changing amount of light and heat from the sun as it follows its yearly path around the sun. These changes give us our seasons. They also give astronomers four convenient points for dividing the year: the summer and winter solstices (the dates with the most and the least daylight hours) and the spring and fall equinoxes (the dates when day and night are of equal length).

Unfortunately for makers of calendars, the earth does not orbit the sun in exactly one year. It actually takes about 365 and one-fourth days. To make up for this difference, we add a day to the calendar every fourth year.

None of these facts makes earth anything special among the planets. But earth has two things that make it unique. For one, it has more water in liquid form than any other planet—not as ice and not as vapor in the atmosphere. And without liquid water, falling as rain, running in streams, and surging in the sea, there can be no life as we know it. Life on earth began in the water, and no living organism on earth can get along entirely without it.

The other unique thing about earth is its atmosphere, which is about 78 percent nitrogen, 21 percent oxygen, and 0.03 percent carbon dioxide, with traces of other substances. No other planet has so much free oxygen in its atmosphere. And, like liquid water, oxygen is vital to life as we know it. Only a few kinds of bacteria can get along without oxygen.

Life and the atmosphere seem to have evolved together. At first, scientists believe, earth's atmosphere had no oxygen—it was composed of hydrogen and helium, the commonest elements in the universe. But earth's gravity was too weak to hold these light gases, and they drifted off into space. New gases appeared from within the earth itself, belched out in volcanic eruptions or leaking through cracks in the crust. Ammonia, water vapor, methane, and carbon dioxide were the main gases of this new atmosphere.

In time, earth's surface cooled down enough so that the water vapor could condense, forming the first oceans. Gases from the atmosphere dissolved in the water, and ultraviolet radiation from the sun knocked them about so that they joined to form giant molecules. These giant molecules were like the stuff that living proteins are made of. The giant molecules had a strange ability to reproduce themselves. They began to behave like semiliving organisms, feeding on the "soup" of chemicals in the water and on each other.

Eventually the first true living cells appeared in the primeval ocean. This happened about 3.4 billion years ago—at least fossil one-celled organisms have been found in rocks this old. About 2 billion years ago a new type of one-celled organism appeared—the first green plants. These made their own food by breaking down carbon dioxide and using the carbon to build energy-rich compounds. As they did this, they released oxygen. Gradually the amount of oxygen in the earth's atmosphere increased, until there was enough to allow more advanced forms of life to evolve. New kinds of many-celled animals and plants appeared by the hundreds about 570,000,000 years ago. Growing steadily more complex and efficient, animals and plants invaded the land. Insects, birds, and mammals developed. As each new form appeared, it took its place in an intricate, interdependent web of life.

Earth is the only planet we know firsthand, and we know much more about earth than about any other planet. But not until the Space Age could we imagine how earth would look from the outside. Color photos taken by satellites show a blue planet, partly covered by swirls and masses of white clouds. (The blue color comes not from the water of the oceans, but from dust and water vapor in the atmosphere, which break up the white sunlight and reflect back the blue rays.) Astronauts who looked down on earth from their orbiting spacecraft have said that it looked like a jewel in space. For the first time they truly realized how precious the earth is, for it is the only planet man can live on naturally. If we want to continue living on this planet, we must not ruin it by wasting its natural resources, polluting its air and water, and ravaging it with wars. There is only one earth.

Eclipse

Eclipse is a phenomenon that occurs when an opaque body passes before a source of light, such as the sun, cutting off the light temporarily. The word *eclipse* comes from the Greek word *ekleipsis*, a form of *ekleipein*, "to fail to appear." This is really a rather mild way of describing an eclipse, where one moment the sun or moon is shining as usual and the next moment begins to disappear.

To primitive people an eclipse was a thing of terror. The moon or worse yet, the sun, was being devoured by some evil monster. If their prayers and sacrifices did not force the monster to vomit up the heavenly body, the end of the world was surely at hand. Even to modern people with a good knowledge of science a solar eclipse is an awesome experience. The sun's light becomes dim and ghastly. Birds stop singing. A dreadful hush seems to settle over the world. Even in a crowded city, traffic slows down and people stop in the streets to steal a quick glance at the darkened sun (however, it should be noted that looking at an eclipse is very bad for your eyes).

In ancient civilizations, the priests kept their knowledge that eclipses were natural happenings to themselves in order to hold their power over the common people. Of course, if only the priests could foretell the darkening of the sun or moon, they must be powerful indeed and it was best to obey them. They alone knew the will of the gods.

Ancient religions had various explanations for eclipses. In Scandinavia, for instance, people believed that a giant wolf was forever chasing the sun and moon. Sometimes it caught up with one or the other and swallowed it. However, the gods always came to the rescue in the nick of time. Some peoples believed that a snake or crocodile swallowed the heavenly body. Primitive peoples beat drums and shrieked loudly to frighten the monster into giving up the sun or moon. More civilized ones prayed fervently.

Actually an eclipse is a very simple natural phenomenon. A solar (sun) eclipse occurs when the moon passes between the sun and the earth, casting a deep shadow on the earth's surface. A lunar (moon) eclipse takes place when the earth passes between the sun and the moon, and the earth's shadow darkens the moon.

An eclipse depends on the three bodies being in line, and this occurs only at certain points in their orbits. Since these positions can be worked out mathematically, eclipses can be predicted accurately for many years in advance. An eclipse may be total or partial, depending on the relative positions of sun, moon, and earth, and on the position of an observer (yourself, for example) on earth.

In a total eclipse of the sun, the moon hides the sun completely from people on the earth along a path about seventy miles wide. People in a zone several hundred miles wide on either side of this path see the sun partly darkened.

Since the moon's shadow races very swiftly across earth's surface, the eclipse can last only about eight minutes at most, and usually much less.

Solar eclipses occur at new moon. They are more common than lunar eclipses—there are about three solar eclipses for every two lunar ones. Up to seven eclipses a year may occur, but three at most will be moon eclipses. There may be as few as two, in which case they will both be of the sun.

Although solar eclipses are more common than lunar eclipses, a person in any one place will see more lunar eclipses than solar ones during his life. The reason is that the shadow cast by earth is much wider than the shadow cast by the moon. A lunar eclipse can be seen by everyone on the dark side of earth, and it can last as long as an hour and a half. But even in a total lunar eclipse the moon does not disappear entirely from sight. The reason is that some rays of sunlight are bent by earth's atmosphere into the shadow path and strike the moon, lighting it with a faint, coppery glow.

Eclipses were probably the earliest astronomical phenomena to be studied. About 4,000 years ago the Chaldeans and Babylonians had worked out the cycle of eclipses, which they called the *saros*, so that they were able to make fairly close predictions of eclipses. The saros was 18 years and 11 days long, and it is still useful for making rough calculations.

Fairly frequently the moon eclipses a star or planet, and occasionally a planet eclipses a star. Such eclipses usually go unnoticed except by sky-watchers with telescopes, because their effect on the sky is so small and so brief. They are called occultations, from the Latin *occultus*, a form of the word *occulere*, "to cover up." And as all students of the occult know, occult means "hidden"—from all but those who know the secret of where to look.

Fomalhaut

Fomalhaut is the bright star that marks the snout of the constellation Piscis Austrinus, the Southern Fish. This constellation is not part of Pisces, but lies near it in the sky. Fomalhaut's name comes by way of Spanish from the Arabic name *Fum-al-Hut*, "Mouth of the Fish." Some astronomy handbooks tell you that Fomalhaut should be pronounced *Fo-mal-o*. This would be fine if we were speaking French, but the correct English pronunciation is *Fo-mal-hawt*, to rhyme with *taught* and *caught*.

Astronomers in bygone centuries created wildly imaginative spellings of the name. Some of them were Phomahant, Fumalhandt, Fomalcuti, and Fontabant.

By any of its names or spellings, Fomalhaut is one of the twenty-five brightest stars visible from earth. A southern star, it hangs low on the horizon in the latitude of New York. But in the latitude of Buenos Aires, Argentina, Cape Town, South Africa, and Canberra, Australia, at certain times of the year it is directly overhead.

Five thousand years ago Fomalhaut was directly on the line of the winter solstice, which made it an important calendar star. Ancient Persian star-worshipers called it one of the Four Guardians of Heaven. The Phoenicians, who lived along the coast of Palestine and Lebanon, identified the bright star, symbolic of water, with their chief god, Dagon, a semihumanoid creature who was half fish.

Some of the early Arab astronomers had different ideas about what Fomalhaut should be. One of them called it the Ostrich. Another called it The First Frog—probably the only time a frog has been set in the stars among gods and heroes.

Galaxy

Galaxy comes from the Greek word *galaxias*, from *gala*, "milk." *Galaxy*, "the milky thing," was first used as a name for the Milky Way, which is a densely packed belt of stars that meanders across the sky like a river of spilled milk. Our own solar system is part of an enormous group of stars that includes the Milky Way. Astronomers call this group of stars the galaxy, but the universe also contains millions of other star groups that rank as galaxies.

Interstellar distances are so vast that with the unaided eye we can see only a few of the stars in our own galaxy. The nearer stars (relatively speaking) form the familiar patterns we know as the constellations. Modern astronomers believe that the Milky Way galaxy contains about 100 *billion* stars, arranged in a huge, flat spiral. The white streak of the Milky Way itself is what we see when we look toward the center of our galaxy, where most of the stars are.

Galaxies could be described as island universes, each containing many millions of stars and planets, plus gas and dust. Millions of galaxies are scattered through space, some of them visible with the aid of telescopes, others detectable only by radio telescope. To the naked eye, the nearest galaxies look like small, faintly glowing clouds among the stars. Formerly they were called nebulas (*nebula* is the Latin word for "cloud"). But modern astronomers distinguish these cloudlike galaxies from true nebulas, which are unimaginably vast clouds of gas and tiny dust particles floating in space within our own Milky Way galaxy.

Ancient and primitive peoples had many stories to explain the Milky Way. The Greeks thought it was the main street of heaven, where all the most important gods had their palaces. The Sumerians, thousands of years before the Greeks, believed the Milky Way was a giant serpent that lay coiled around the world with its tail in its mouth. Norsemen and some American Indians believed it was the path that the souls of dead warriors followed to their celestial rewards. The Babylonians and Mongols speculated that it was the seam where the two halves of the universe were sewed together. In Hindu legend, the Milky Way is the former bed of the Ganges River, which once flowed across the heavens but fell to earth and became one of the holy places of India. Polynesian mythmakers said that it was a great shark-spirit that swam through the sky devouring clouds. Some American Indian tribes had the pleasant idea that the Milky Way was a path of glowing-hot ashes placed in the sky to help late travelers find their way home.

Gemini

Gemini is the third constellation in the zodiac. Its name is Latin for "Twins," and it commemorates the mythical twins Castor and Pollux.

As the Greeks told the story, Zeus fell in love with Leda, the wife of one of the Kings of Sparta. Transforming himself into a swan, he made love to her on the bank of a river. After this extremely strange mating, Leda laid a giant egg from which were hatched three children: Castor, Pollux, and Helen of Troy.

Castor was mortal and Pollux was immortal, but the two brothers were devoted to each other. When they grew up, Castor became famous as a soldier and tamer of horses. Pollux was the world's best boxer. Helen grew up to be the most beautiful woman in the world, and the legendary cause of the Trojan War. But her story is really a very different one from that of her brothers.

The Twins' names are rather interesting. *Castor* means "beaver." *Pollux* (short for Polydeuces) means "much sweet wine." The two were said to look exactly alike, except that Pollux had boxing scars on his face. The twins fought victoriously in many battles, wearing eggshell caps (in honor of their strange birth) and riding snow-white horses. They took part in the Trojan War and helped to bring their runaway sister Helen back to Sparta. But eventually they met their match in another set of supernatural twins. In a grudge fight with these, Castor was killed. Pollux tried to kill himself in his grief but could not die, since he was immortal. He prayed to Zeus and refused his immortality if he could not share it with his beloved brother. Zeus, impressed by this brotherly love, which was so different from the relationship between him and his own brothers, agreed to let the Twins take turns living on Mount Olympus among the gods and in the Underworld among the unhappy ghosts of the dead. As a further reward he set their images in the sky as the constellation Gemini, marked by the two brilliant stars we call Castor and Pollux.

The Greeks were not alone in thinking of these stars as twins. The Hindus called them the Asvins, twin god-warriors mounted on horses. Polynesian islanders in the middle of the Pacific Ocean, who had never heard of either Greeks or Hindus, also thought of them as twins. The primitive Bushmen, wandering hunters of South Africa, thought they were two young women, wives of a giant antelope-god.

The Egyptians thought of the Twins as two sprouting plants. Centuries later, the Arabs called them Twin Peacocks. In Jewish tradition the Twins were sometimes identified with the tribes of Simeon and Levi.

But they were most important to the Greeks and Romans, who actually believed that the Twins led them in battle. They were guardian spirits of Sparta and of Rome, and soldiers prayed to them before a battle. Sailors also prayed to them, for they were said to rescue shipwrecked seamen. They also had the power to send favorable winds.

The Twins were so much in the minds of Romans that "by Gemini!" was one of the commonest Roman oaths. It survives today as "jiminy!" Many an American who says "by jiminy" doesn't know that he is really calling on the pagan half-gods Castor and Pollux.

In the sky, the most noticeable feature of Gemini is the stars Castor and Pollux. A line of four or five less bright stars trails behind each. Greenish-white Castor is a multiple star with six components, all revolving around a common center. Orange-colored Pollux also contains six stars. Castor was formerly brighter than Pollux, but now Pollux is brighter.

In astrology, Gemini is ruled by the planet Mercury. Its lucky day is Wednesday, its gem is the emerald, and its lucky numbers are three and four. Gemini people are supposed to be bright, intellectual, and have a talent for science. Arthur Conan Doyle, the author who created Sherlock Holmes, was born under Gemini. So were the comedian Bob Hope, the glamorous actress Marilyn Monroe, Britain's stodgy Queen Victoria, and Jefferson Davis, the president of the Confederate States of America.

Jupiter

Jupiter, the largest planet of the solar system and the fifth from the sun, is named for the chief of the Roman gods. Jupiter was a sky god, corresponding to the Greeks' Zeus, and eventually he took over all the myths about Zeus in addition to some of his own. Jupiter, whose original name was probably "Diaus Pitar," meaning "Sky Father," controlled the weather and the thunder and lightning. Sometimes he controlled men's and women's fates, but usually he did not intervene. Although he was the most powerful of all the gods, he had a hard time controlling the other gods, for they were an unruly set of supernatural powers.

Another name for Jupiter was Jove, which Englishmen still use as a mild oath. The adjective *jovial* means "jolly" or "good-humored." It comes from an old belief that people born under the sign of Jupiter/Jove have happy, fun-loving dispositions.

The planet Jupiter is a giant sphere of gas, probably with a small, solid core. It is about eleven times the diameter of earth and contains almost 320 times as much matter. In fact, astronomers calculate that Jupiter contains almost two and a half times as much matter as all the other planets put together. Jupiter is made up mostly of hydrogen and helium, which are the two most abundant substances in the solar system. The planet can hold these very light substances because of its immensely powerful gravity and its low temperature, which has been measured at about −240° F (−150° C) at the outer edge of its atmosphere.

Jupiter is not a perfect sphere. It is more like a slightly squashed beach ball. The planet's swift rotation (nearly 2.5 times as fast as earth's) makes it bulge out at the equator and flattens it slightly at the poles.

Jupiter is covered by swirling clouds of frozen ammonia, hundreds of miles deep, which hide its surface completely. Beneath the clouds, astronomers believe, is a thick layer of frozen water vapor. Then comes a layer of hydrogen and helium—about15,000 miles (25,000 kilometers) thick—forced into liquid form by the great pressure of the planet's gravity. The next layer down is hydrogen and helium that have been squeezed still further, into the form of a liquid metal. This layer may be as much as 28,000 miles (45,000 kilometers) thick. Then, astronomers think, comes the core, composed mainly of iron and silicon. The whole planet is wrapped in a wide, very thinly spread-out blanket of hydrogen and helium gases.

To the naked eye Jupiter looks serene and slightly yellow, but a telescope reveals that its atmosphere is very turbulent. Alternate bright and dark bands, parallel to the Jovian equator, cover most of the planet's area. Color photos taken by the space probe *Pioneer X* showed that the bright bands were pale gray, white, or yellow, while the dark bands were orange or reddish-brown. The bands are constantly shifting, melting into one another, and reappearing.

Jupiter's most famous feature is probably the Great Red Spot, which covers an area larger than any continent on earth. The Great Red Spot varies in color from brick red to pink to gray. Like the bands of the atmosphere, it shrinks and expands, and sometimes disappears entirely. The Great Red Spot was discovered more than three hundred years ago, but until recently astronomers were not certain of what it was. In 1973 the space probe *Pioneer X* flew past Jupiter and radioed pictures and data back to earth. The evidence seems to show that the Great Red Spot is an atmospheric disturbance, something like a titanic hurricane.

In some ways Jupiter behaves more like a star than a planet. It gives off powerful radio waves. It also gives off more energy than it receives from the sun. Astronomers are puzzled by this, for Jupiter does not have nearly enough mass for the kind of thermonuclear reaction that fuels stars. Also, it was believed that the giant planet was too cold for any sort of nuclear reaction. However, data from *Pioneer X* hint that the temperature at the core of Jupiter may be almost 54,000° F (30,000° C)—nearly six times as hot as the surface of the sun.

Jupiter takes almost twelve earth years to complete one revolution around the sun, but it spins so fast on its axis that a day and night together last less than ten earth hours. Thirteen moons brighten Jupiter's nights; one of them is larger than the planet Mercury. Late in 1975 a scientist in California announced that he had discovered a fourteenth moon, using special photographic equipment and a 200-inch telescope. He needed this help, because the fourteenth moon is only four miles in diameter.

To ancient astrologers Jupiter was known as the King of the Planets. It was thought to affect the mystical workings of whatever sign of the zodiac it was in—it passes to a new one about every twelve months. According to astrological lore, Jupiter rules the sign of Sagittarius and is known as the God of Fortune. It is said to give generosity, benevolence, and happiness—or else wastefulness, impatience, and lawlessness. The astrologers cover all the bets.

Leo

Leo, the Lion, is the fifth constellation of the zodiac. Its name is the Latin word for "lion," although the star-group does not look much like a lion. In fact, its most noticeable stars look like a sickle or a backwards-turned question mark. But Leo has been associated with lions since very early times. The reason is almost certainly that about 5,000 years ago Leo was the constellation in which the sun rose at the summer solstice. The Middle Eastern sun in summertime is fierce and destroying. The fierce, powerful lion was an apt symbol for it. Indeed, in ancient times the lion was one of the four beast-gods that ruled the seasons of the year.

The Sumerians were the first civilization to name Leo as a constellation and link it with the lion's mystical powers. Later civilizations followed suit. Old zodiacs from India and Egypt show Leo very much as it is pictured in Mediterranean star maps. The Arabs were so impressed by the idea of a lion constellation that they drew up a superlion that spread over nearly half the sky.

In Greek mythology, Leo was the Nemean Lion, a beast of monstrous size whose mother was the moon. The Lion dropped to earth as a shooting star, and immediately began attacking and devouring everything in sight. It had eaten all the people and livestock of a large area of Greece when Hercules was ordered to destroy it.

Hercules was a half-god—he was one of Zeus' uncountable children—and he had superhuman strength. Even so, he had great difficulty in disposing of the lion. Its hide could not be pierced by any sort of weapon. When Hercules threw spears at it, they glanced off harmlessly. When he chopped at it with his great sword, the heavy blade bent like soft aluminum foil. At last Hercules had to chase the beast into a cave and choke it to death. Afterwards, he skinned the lion with its own sharp claws and used the hide for armor. The head he wore as a helmet. After Hercules' death, the lion's skin was nailed up in the sky as a trophy.

Most early civilizations thought of Leo as a lionlike creature—even the Incas in Peru thought it was a puma springing on its prey. But the Chinese pictured it as the Horse in their zodiac. The stars of Leo's sickle-shaped head could just as easily be a horse with arched neck as a lion's head and mane.

Leo has one very bright star, Regulus, whose name is Latin for "little king." As long ago as 3000 B.C. people of the Middle East believed that Regulus ruled the other stars of the sky and kept them in order. The Persians called it one of the Four Royal Stars. Blue-white Regulus is one of the twenty-five brightest stars; it gives off about one hundred times as much light as the sun.

In astrology Leo symbolizes strength, courage, and fire, and is said to rule the heart. Old English astrologers believed that people born under Leo were destined for riches, power, and glory. (Poor, undistinguished Leos obviously were not counted.) Leo's lucky gem is the ruby; the lucky day is Sunday; the lucky numbers are five and nine; the lucky colors are gold and orange. The great French general Napoleon was born under Leo.

Libra

Libra, the seventh constellation of the zodiac, is named from the Latin word for a set of scales or balances—the ancient kind that has a pan hanging from each end of a beam. The beam is hung up by its middle, and whatever is to be weighed goes into one pan. Weights are added gradually to the other pan until both pans hang level and even. *Libra* also means the old Roman pound weight, which was 12 ounces (340 grams).

The shape of Libra vaguely suggests an old-time balance scale. It certainly impressed the astronomers of several civilizations that way: Chinese, Hindu, Jewish, and Syrian, to mention a few. The Egyptians identified Libra with the Nilometer, which measured the height of the Nile's yearly floods. They believed that the constellation stopped the flow of water when the river was high enough.

The Egyptians also believed that Libra symbolized the scales in which every human soul was weighed after death. The great god Osiris supervised the weighing, and the dog-headed god Anubis handled the scales. Into one pan went the soul, and into the other went the Feather of Truth. If the soul were lighter than the feather, it went to heaven. If its sins made it heavier than the feather, it was sent to the Underworld to be punished.

The ancient Greeks, however, saw Libra as the claws of Scorpio, and in the West it was not considered a constellation in its own right until about 50 B.C. It was the Romans who turned the Scorpion's Claws into the heavenly Scales—at least, they took credit for it.

The Romans connected Libra with the Goddess of Justice, Astraea, who was pictured as weighing each person's case in her balance. On a more practical level, Roman farmers used Libra as the signal to sow grain in the fall, to live over the winter and ripen for the harvest in spring. At the time when Libra was declared a constellation, it marked the autumn equinox, when night and day are equal. Roman astronomers may have thought of Libra as balancing the days against the nights.

In astrology, Libra is ruled by Venus. The lucky day for Librans is Friday; the lucky numbers are six and nine; the lucky color is pastel blue. Librans are said to have very good judgment. They are also said to be idealistic but seldom put their high ideals into practice. The same can be said for plenty of people born under every sign of the zodiac.

Mars

Mars, the red planet, is named for the Roman God of War. Far back in history, before Rome was founded, Mars seems to have been a god of the forests that then covered Italy and of the crops that the half-civilized Italian tribes raised in their forest clearings. By the time Rome was founded, as a fortified hilltop village forever quarreling with its neighbors, Mars had also become a warrior god. Roman farmers had to be ready at all times to fight off enemy raids on their herds and crops, when they weren't out themselves raiding nearby villages.

Mars' original name was Mavors, later cut down to Mars. He was also called Mamers, Marmar, and Marspiter. His season lasted from March (the month of Mars) to mid-October, from sowing to harvesting. These were also the months for making war—in the winter the weather was too bad, and people stayed home. His sacred animals were the wolf, the woodpecker, and the horse, which was used only in warfare in the early days of Rome.

Mars was not a very popular god in ancient Rome. He had few temples. However, he had a shrine in the former royal palace where his sacred spears were kept. Before beginning a war, the highest official of the Roman Republic would enter the shrine and shake the spears, shouting, "Mars, WAKE UP!" If the spears moved by themselves, it was a sign that the war-god was angry and needed a big sacrifice to put him back in a good mood. (Of course, only the man who entered the room knew whether the spears really moved or not.) Mars first became a popular god about the time Jesus was born, when the emperor Augustus built him a magnificent new temple in Rome and pushed his worship.

When Rome conquered Greece, the Romans identified Mars with the Greek war-god Ares. They forgot the myths about Mars—or maybe he never had very many—and gave him Ares' myths instead. Ares was a drunken, quarrelsome, overbearing god who loved fighting and killing for their own sakes. All the other gods hated him except for his sister Eris, who scurried around the world stirring up quarrels, Aphrodite, who was stupidly in love with him, and Hades, Lord of the Dead, who was grateful for all the new subjects Ares was continually sending him.

The planet Mars is one of the five visible to the naked eye; so the people of ancient times knew it well. The Sumerians were probably the first to identify it with the god of war, because it is red—the color of a slain foeman's blood, or the flames of a burning village. Later peoples followed this belief.

Philosophers and astrologers credited Mars with powerful influences on man's fate. Mars is said to rule the signs of Aries and Scorpio, which once marked the beginning and end of the war season.

The scientific study of the planet Mars began in 1609, when Galileo first observed it through a telescope. Mars is the fourth planet from the sun. It is about 4,200 miles in diameter (6,787 kilometers), which is a little over half the diameter of earth. But it has only about one tenth of the mass of earth because it contains less of the heavy elements. As a result, its gravity is much weaker—only thirty-eight percent as strong as earth's. On Mars, a 200-pound (91 kilograms) football player would weigh only 76 pounds (34.5 kilograms). But all the other players would be just as much lighter; so everything would be even. The football field would have to be lengthened, however, because a pass or kick would travel much further than it would on earth.

About every two years and seven weeks, Mars' orbit brings it relatively close to earth. Every fifteen to seventeen years the two planets come their closest, within 35 million miles of each other. The closer Mars is, the brighter it appears in the sky, and the more details can be seen with a telescope. Most of what we know about the surface of Mars, however, comes from a series of spacecraft, all named *Mariner*, that orbited the planet in the late 1960s and early 1970s and radioed photographs and other information back to earth.

Mars has two moons, named Deimos and Phobos (Greek for "Terror" and "Fear," respectively). They are so small that they cannot be seen without a powerful telescope—Phobos, the inner moon, is only 10 or 12 miles (16–19 kilometers) wide at its greatest measurement, and Deimos is about half that size. They are shaped like battered potatoes. Their existence was predicted as early as 1610, but they were not discovered until 1877.

To the naked eye, Mars looks bright red. But color photos

from the *Mariner* space probes show that it is really rusty-orange and gray, with white caps at the poles. The orange color is probably caused by iron oxide, created when oxygen that was once in the Martian atmosphere combined with iron in the rocks of the planet's crust.

The atmosphere of Mars is very thin, only one percent as dense as earth's. The pressure at ground level on Mars is equal to the pressure at 20 miles (32 kilometers) up in earth's atmosphere. Human beings could not live a second on Mars without pressurized suits and a breathing supply. Most of the atmosphere is composed of carbon dioxide, with small amounts of nitrogen and water vapor. Some astronomers believe that Mars once had an atmosphere much more like earth's. But the red planet's weak gravity let most of the atmosphere drift off into space.

Thin as the Martian atmosphere is, it has fierce winds of as much as 150 miles (240 kilometers) per hour, which whip up great clouds of yellow dust that hide much of the planet's surface. There are also white clouds, probably of frozen water vapor, and blue clouds, whose nature is still unknown.

The atmosphere is not dense enough to serve as an insulating blanket, as earth's does; so the temperature on Mars swings wildly up by day and down by night. Just after noon on the Martian equator, the temperature reaches 80°F (27° C). At night it drops to −4° (−20° C) at the equator. At the poles, the nighttime temperature drops as low as −200° F (−129° C).

The polar caps appear to be a mixture of frozen carbon dioxide and water in the form of hoarfrost. They are probably no more than two or three feet (0.6–0.9 meters) thick. The polar caps shrink in the Martian spring and grow again in the fall. As they shrink, dark areas spread out around them as if they were melting and releasing water to Mars' bone-dry, dusty soil. There is still no proof, however, that this is what really happens.

Because of Mars' turbulent atmosphere and dust clouds, our ideas about the Martian surface were once based largely on guesswork. But photos from *Mariner 9*, which orbited the red planet in 1972, revealed mountains taller than any on earth, vast plains, gigantic canyons, and thousands of craters.

The most argued-about features of Mars are the so-called canals. In 1877 an Italian astronomer named Schiaparelli looked through his telescope and saw what appeared to be long, straight lines radiating out from the polar caps. The lines swam in and out of focus in a tantalizing and confusing manner. But Schiaparelli was sure enough of what he'd seen to publish a report. He called the mysterious lines *canali*, Italian for "channels." Unfortunately, this was translated into most European languages, including English, as "canals"— waterways planned and dug by intelligent beings—which was not what Schiaparelli meant at all.

Other astronomers had a great deal of trouble verifying what, if anything, Schiaparelli had seen because of the difficulty of getting a clear view of the Martian surface. A great American astronomer, Percival Lowell, at first pooh-poohed Schiaparelli's "canals." But one night he was amazed to see them fleetingly through his own telescope. Lowell was converted and became a firm believer in the canals. He believed that he saw them many times afterwards. Indeed he went so far as to assert that they were proof that civilized beings existed on Mars, for only civilized beings could cooperate to plan and build such mighty waterways.

The argument went on, pro and con, for years, until photos

from *Mariner 9* brought new evidence. There are no canals. But there are long, narrow, nearly straight zones formed by some kind of land feature. Some are probably cracks in the planet's crust; others may be valleys cut by streams of water long ago.

Although canals never existed on Mars, there are signs that at some time in Mars' past there was plenty of water. *Mariner 9's* photos show long twisting valleys that look like dried-up river beds. Some of them are linked in complex patterns that look like the patterns of river systems on earth, as seen from an orbiting spacecraft.

For many years earthmen have been intrigued by the possibility that life may exist on Mars. The discovery of the "canals" made it more exciting than ever. In 1898 an English writer named H. G. Wells came out with a novel called *The War of the Worlds.* In it he described in great detail how spiderlike creatures from Mars invaded earth in spaceships. Armed with superweapons, they devastated the unprepared earthlings right and left—until rescue came in the form of earth disease germs that killed them off. Wells' novel was a real shocker for the well-bred, stuffy England of 1898, and it soon became a best-seller. It is still one of the classics of science fiction.

But is there really life on Mars? The chances do not look good, for the Martian environment is so harsh. Any form of life that exists on Mars must be able to get along without free oxygen and without liquid water. It must also be able to stand a daily temperature range of about 180° F (100° C) at the warmest part of Mars, or somewhat less near the poles. And it must be able to withstand ultraviolet radiations that would be deadly for earth life. Nevertheless, many astronomers believe that life capable of existing under such conditions could have evolved on Mars, and that it exists there now.

If there are living organisms on Mars, they are probably one-celled, like bacteria, or simple plants like lichens. If there are any larger organisms, we might not even recognize them as being alive, so strange would they be to our eyes. Nevertheless, scientists take the possibility of life on Mars so seriously that the United States launched two robot spacecraft, Viking I in August 1975, and Viking II in September 1975, to land on Mars in 1976, examine the soil for evidence of life, and radio back data.

Can Mars ever become a colony for some of earth's overcrowded population? This is a question being seriously asked by scientists. To exist on Mars, humans would need artificial environments where they could breathe and the temperature could be kept livable. The lack of water would be a serious problem, but many astronomers believe that there is a layer of permanently frozen water a few feet below the surface of Mars. This water could be mined and used. Using solar power, nuclear power, or perhaps harnessing the fierce Martian winds to electric generators, the colonists could extract oxygen from the rocks, or from the carbon dioxide of the Martian atmosphere. Green plants raised in tanks of nutrient solution could supply food and also recycle precious oxygen. Fantastic? Yes, but so were airplanes and television once.

Mercury

Mercury, the smallest planet in the solar system and the one closest to the sun, is named for the Roman god Mercury. This god began as the protector of merchants (his name came from *merx*, or "merchandise"). Later on he was identified with the Greek god Hermes, messenger of the gods, who was also the god of thieves, eloquence, skill, and roads, as well as of traders. Perhaps the speed with which the little planet scoots past the sun suggested a fleeing thief.

Mercury is very hard to observe. Most people have never seen it. Most of the time it is either hidden behind the sun or invisible in the sun's glare. However, for several days in spring and fall it can be seen just after sunset and just before sunrise, low on the horizon. Thirteen times every century, Mercury crosses the face of the sun as seen from earth. If the planet were big enough, it would cause an eclipse. But it is so small—only 3,025 miles (4,800 kilometers) in diameter—that it can be seen only through a telescope, like a small, black ball rolling across the sun.

Mercury keeps the same side always toward the sun as it swings around its orbit. This makes the sunny side hot enough to melt lead, while the dark side is nearly 300 degrees below zero F ($-185°$ C). Photos and other data sent back to earth by the space probe *Mariner 10* show that Mercury has no atmosphere. The planet's surface is like the Moon's—rugged mountains and wide, level plains, pitted with craters—some created by volcanoes and others made by meteorites smashing into the planet's crust. A space probe landing on Mercury could tell us much more about this mysterious planet, but no instruments yet built would work for long in the extreme heat of Mercury's sunny side or the bitter cold of its dark side.

In astrology, Mercury rules the signs of Gemini and Virgo. It is supposed to rule the mind and memory. When it is favorable, the mind is clear and works efficiently. When it is unfavorable, the person ruled by it should be careful when signing contracts and be sure not to quarrel with relatives, neighbors, and fellow workers. The warning against signing contracts must surely come from the time when Mercury was worshipped as the god of businessmen and thieves.

Meteor

Meteor comes from the Greek *meteora* meaning "atmospheric phenomena," or in plainer language, anything going on in the air. *Meteora* is a form of the adjective *meteoros*, meaning "raised up" or "lofty," so another way of saying it would be "things up there." To the Greeks, a "meteor" could be a cloud, rain, snow, hail, wind, lightning, and so on. This is why the science that deals with weather and the atmosphere is known today as meteorology. A "meteor" could also be a star, a planet, or one of those mysterious streaks of fire in the night sky known as "shooting stars."

In astronomy, a meteor means the streak of light seen in the sky when a solid body from space enters earth's atmosphere and the friction of the air heats it up glowing hot. It can also mean the chunk of matter that produces the phenomenon. But modern astronomers, trying to be precise, call the chunk of matter a meteoroid.

Most meteoroids are only the size of a grain of sand or a small pebble, and even this is enough to make a streak of light, but some weigh many tons. Perhaps once in 10,000 years a supergiant meteoroid the size of a small mountain may strike the earth, punching out a huge crater. The famous Meteor Crater in Arizona, for example, measures about 4,000 feet (1,220 meters) across and 570 feet (174 meters) deep, with a pushed-up rim around it that looms 160 feet (49 meters) above the surrounding desert plain. But most meteoroids vaporize high in the atmosphere from the heat of friction, before they get within 25 miles (40 kilometers) of earth's surface. When the vaporized meteoroid material cools down, it solidifies as dust, which gradually drifts down to the ground. Several thousand tons of meteor material fall on earth each day.

Meteoroids that get all the way to earth's surface without being vaporized are called meteorites. Most meteorites consist of a natural iron-nickel alloy that is hard, tough, and rust-resistant. Others are heavy stone with a good deal of iron and nickel in it. Some scientists believe that the first iron that man ever used came from meteorites. About one to ten meteorites big enough to notice reach earth daily, scattered all over the globe. Most are small. In earlier times people used to call them "thunderstones," believing them to be petrified lightning bolts such as the various gods and demons of the air threw at each other.

The larger meteoroids are probably chunks of asteroids that have disintegrated. The small ones appear to come from comets. Astronomers believe they are bits of sand and gravel that have been torn loose from a comet's nucleus and drift through space until they encounter a planet. Several times a year earth passes through a belt of meteoroids, producing some spectacular atmospheric fireworks known as meteor showers. Ancient records speak of stars falling like rain, though the average meteor shower is not that spectacular. During a meteor shower as many as 60 meteors per hour may be seen. But even without meteor showers about 200 million meteors capable of producing a flash enter the atmosphere every twenty-four hours. Many of them are not seen because they occur during daylight, and only a very small fraction of the number can be seen from any one place.

More meteors are seen after midnight than before. The reason is that up to midnight, the only meteors that can enter the atmosphere are those that are going in the same direction as earth in its orbit around the sun. This means that they must catch up, and a great many never do. After midnight, the turning earth scoops up masses of meteoroids coming in the opposite direction, like a great whale swimming through a mass of plankton with its mouth wide open.

A meteor that is especially large, bright, and long-lasting is called a fireball. "Ball of fire" is a slangy expression for a very energetic, go-getting sort of person. It is interesting to speculate whether this may originally have meant an over-heated chunk of rock from outer space.

Moon

Moon comes from the Anglo-Saxon word *mona*, which comes from a very ancient root meaning "to measure." The Anglo-Saxons like many other people from the beginning of history down to modern times, used the moon as their chief measure of time. The moon's regular waxing (growing) and waning (shrinking) made it a wonderful timekeeper for people who had no calendars and no writing and who lived a slow-paced life based on hunting or farming.

The earliest civilizations used the moon as the basis of their calendars, and to this day the Jewish religious calendar, the Muslim calendar, and the traditional Chinese calendar are based on the moon. Each new moon begins a new month. The word *month* itself comes from *moon*, and in parts of Europe people once spoke of the "moon of plowing," the "moon of haying," and so on. American Indians gave us names like "hunters' moon" and "harvest moon."

The proper adjective for the moon is *lunar*, which comes from *luna*, the Latin name for the moon. Language experts think *luna* came from an older word, *lucsna*, which meant "the shining one." The ancient Greeks called the moon *selene*, from the word *selas*, meaning "bright." Strangely enough, the moon is considered masculine in some languages and feminine in others.

This comes down to us from the long-past times when the moon was worshiped as a god or goddess. The ancient Babylonians thought of the moon as a male god, the husband of the sun. The Greeks worshiped the same moon as a triple goddess who ruled the stages of women's lives from birth to death. The Hindus believed the moon was king of the sky and the husband of twenty-seven beautiful stars. The Egyptians believed the moon was a sailor-god named Khonsu, who piloted his shining boat through the sky. In Christian times, the moon became a symbol of the Virgin Mary.

The real moon is a far cry from the gods and goddesses the ancients imagined it to be. It is an airless, waterless, barren globe of dark gray rock, circling the earth at an average distance of 238,857 miles (384,560 kilometers).

The moon is about one-fourth the diameter of earth, but it has only one-eightieth of the earth's mass. The reason is that the moon is composed mostly of lighter chemical elements than earth. Because of its smaller size and lower density, the moon's gravity is only about one-sixth that of earth, so that a man on the moon can make great, kangaroolike leaps, as the astronauts found out. The moon's gravity is too weak to hold oxygen or any of the other gases that make up an atmosphere, and any water the moon may once have had has long since evaporated and drifted off into space. Because it has no atmosphere to insulate it, the moon has an extremely harsh climate. On its sunny side, the temperature is about 250° F (121° C); on the dark side, which has not yet been explored by astronauts, it probably drops to −112° F (−80° C).

Poets, songwriters, and authors have written countless lines about the mystery and beauty of moonlight. The moon's cold, bluish light is reflected sunlight. In clear weather the full moon is about eighty times as bright as all the visible stars in the sky together. Just after new moon, the moon's dark portion seems to glow with a faint, reddish light. This is sunlight reflected from earth, and it is known as "earthshine."

One of the most noticeable things about the moon is the way it changes from a large, bright disk to a thin sliver of light, goes dark, and then comes back again. This is caused by changes in the relative positions of earth, moon, and sun. When the moon lies directly between earth and sun, the side toward earth gets no light and cannot be seen. This stage is called "new moon." As the moon moves around toward the far side of earth, it begins to reflect sunlight. As we see more and more of its surface, it appears to wax. As our satellite moves around toward the sun once more, it appears to wane.

Since the moon makes just one revolution on its own axis each time it orbits earth, it always keeps the same face turned toward our planet. Actually we can see a little more than half of the moon's face, but not all at the same time. Slight changes in the positions of moon and earth make the moon appear to tilt, bringing additional areas into view at the beginning and end of each orbit.

Superstitious people believe the moon governs people's fates, the weather, the growth of crops, and many other things. It does not, of course, but it does have a tremendously important effect on earth by causing the ocean tides. It also affects many kinds of animal behavior, such as the feeding habits of fish.

To some people, the dark areas on the moon's face seem to show the face of an old man or an old woman, or two lovers kissing. But in many parts of the world people think of them as a rabbit. An Indian tribe on the Northwest coast thought they were a toad. Actually they are huge, low-lying plains called *maria* (Latin for "seas.") The first men to look at the moon through a telescope, in the early sixteen hundreds, thought these huge, dark areas must be bodies of water. But even learned astronomers can be wrong, and today we know that these "seas" are bone-dry. Actually, they were formed by ancient lava flows.

There are probably hundreds of superstitions about the Moon. In parts of England, people once thought it was a sin to point your finger at the moon, and at new moon men touched their hats and girls curtsied to show their respect. Otherwise, they feared, the moon might send them bad luck to punish them for their bad manners. All over Europe, people believed that hair and fingernails should only be cut while the moon is waning. Carpenters in ancient Rome would not use wood cut when the moon was full, claiming that it was sure to rot quickly. European farmers would not kill pigs on a waning moon, believing that the meat would go bad or would shrivel up when it was cooked. The moon's rays were thought to blind people who slept out in the open. One of the best-known moon superstitions was that the light of the moon caused insanity. Our words *lunacy* and *lunatic* come from this old belief.

The English language has many expressions derived from the moon. One of them is *mooncalf,* an old expression for an idiot or an absent-minded person. Another, dating back to Shakespeare's time, is *moonstruck,* meaning distracted, dazed, or otherwise mentally affected by the moon's baneful rays. *To moon about,* still in use, means to mope around, listless and dreary, as if moonstruck.

Moonlighting came into the language in the early 1880s, when it meant the acts of vengeance that poor Irish tenant farmers perpetrated under the cover of night against the rich men who owned their land. Today it has come to mean holding down a second job after one's regular working hours, usually without the boss' knowledge.

From the late 1400s to the late 1800s, *moonshine* meant foolish, empty talk. In the 1780s it took on another meaning: smuggled or illegally made liquor. Both these activities were best carried out by night. The moon gave smugglers and distillers enough light to work without using torches, which could give away their position to the eagerly watching lawmen. It was Englishmen who first used *moonshine* in this sense, but the term quickly leaped the Atlantic, like many another useful import from the British Isles, including the art of making whiskey itself.

To top it off, we have "once in a blue moon," which means very, very rarely, or never. How often have you seen the moon look blue?

Nebula

Nebula is a Latin word meaning "fog" or "cloud." Astronomers use the word to mean a huge "cloud" in space. Some nebulas are clouds of gas and dust. Others are groups of stars—in fact, entire galaxies—so far away that they look like tiny, faint, luminous patches of haze in the sky.

Although man had been watching the stars since pre-historic times, not until the 1720s did he have good enough instruments to detect nebulas in the night sky (except for a few distant galaxies that can be seen with the naked eye). As telescopes improved, more and more nebulas were discovered. Still more showed up when astronomers began to use cameras to take time-exposure photos of the heavens. Many nebulas too faint to make an impression on the human eye—even with a telescope—showed up on film as noticeable patches of light.

Some nebulas reflect the light of millions of stars shining on them; others glow with fluorescent light as they soak up the energy of starlight. Nebulas that are actually made up of stars, of course, shine with their own light. But not all nebulas are light. Some are dark masses of dust and gas that look like ragged black holes in the sky, hiding the stars behind them.

A few of the best-known nebulas are the Crab Nebula in the constellation Taurus; the Horsehead Nebula (a dark nebula) in the Milky Way; and the Great Spirit Nebula in the constellation Andromeda (actually a galaxy) one of the very few nebulas that can be seen with the naked eye.

Astronomers call the gas-and-dust nebulas diffuse nebulas (*diffuse* is a Latin word meaning "spread out"). And in these nebulas the matter is very thinly spread out indeed—more thinly than in the best vacuum man can produce on earth. Nevertheless, many astronomers think these nebulas are the breeding grounds of new stars. According to the "nebular hypothesis," the widely scattered atoms, molecules, and microscopic dust particles of the nebula attract each other and gradually draw closer. The closer they get, the stronger the attraction becomes. Eventually the cloud becomes so tightly packed that it heats up. Nuclear reactions begin, and the cloud gives off light. Natural forces of radiation energy and gravity cause the incandescent cloud to spin, and this makes the outer layers of gas and dust break off. Over millions or billions of years, the large central mass of gas and dust condenses into the super-hot body of matter we call a star. The material in the outer rings breaks up into smaller masses, which shrink and cool down to become planets circling the star. Most astronomers believe our own solar system originated this way.

Neptune

Neptune is the eighth planet from the sun and the fifth planet beyond the earth. Named for the Roman God of the Sea, it is too faint to be seen without a telescope or powerful binoculars, and so it was unknown to the Romans and Greeks. Neptune was not discovered until 1846. Two astronomers, one English and one French, had predicted that an unknown planet existed beyond Uranus, since Uranus' orbit was so erratic that some heavenly body must be affecting it. The planet was actually discovered by a German to whom the Frenchman had sent his calculations. The Englishman, who had cautiously delayed coming out with his theory, missed out on the glory.

Neptune is a giant planet, nearly four times the diameter of earth. In the telescope it shines with a yellow glow, but it is so far from earth that no surface details can be seen, even with the most powerful instrument. Circling the sun at a distance of nearly 2.8 billion miles (4.5 billion kilometers), Neptune takes almost 165 years to complete a single orbit. Its day and night are a little under 8 hours each. No earthman could enjoy a Neptunian day, however. So little heat reaches Neptune from the sun that the planet's surface temperature is about $-360°$ F $(-220°$ C), and the frigid atmosphere is composed of hydrogen, methane, and probably helium, none of which is breathable.

Although Neptune was absolutely unknown to the ancient peoples who invented the art of astrology—they didn't even suspect it existed—modern astrologers have found a place for it. Neptune rules the sign of Pisces—very suitable for a sea-god—and confers the gifts of inspiration and idealism. In its bad aspect, it causes laziness, deceit, shiftlessness, and disrespect—or so astrologers say.

Neptune the god was really the Greek Sea-God Poseidon with a Roman name. Poseidon was one of Zeus' brothers. In additon to being a sea-god, he was also a horse-god and the ruler of all earthquakes. Scholars think he probably began as a river-god. But there are no rivers or oceans on the planet that is named for him. Any water that exists there—astronomers believe that there is a layer of ice 5,000 miles (8,000 kilometers) thick surrounding Neptune's rocky core—is frozen harder than steel.

North Star

North Star, or Pole Star, is the star toward which the Earth's north pole points. More scientifically, the North Star marks the approximate location of the north celestial pole, which is the spot in the heavens at which the north end of the earth's axis points.

Few things would seem to be less changeable than the North Star, steadfastly marking true north when even compasses fail. But in fact the North Star does change. The reason is that the earth's axis is not steady. It wobbles very, very slowly, like a giant top that is slowing down. As it wobbles, its ends—the poles—describe a slow circle in space. Thus the north pole swings gradually away from the Pole Star and toward a new one. Right now the north celestial pole has passed about one half degree beyond the present Pole Star. It takes about 6,500 years to complete the switch to a new Pole Star.

The present North Star is Alpha Ursae Minoris, the brightest star in the Little Bear—or Little Dipper, as we say in the United States. Four thousand years ago it was the star Thuban in the constellation Draco. In 12,000 years it will be Vega. In 26,000 years the earth's axis will have swung around to point at Alpha Ursae Minoris once more.

Another name for the North Star is *Stella Polaris*, Latin for "Star of the Pole." The Anglo-Saxons called it *Scip-Steorre*, or "Ship-Star," for they used it to navigate their ships by. In fact, the North Star was used by seamen of all nations before the compass was invented. In Shakespeare's time it was called the Lodestar (*lode* was an old form of *lead*, and the North Star led ships on their courses).

The North Star is not especially bright, but there is an easy way to locate it by using the Big Dipper. The two end stars in the Dipper's bowl point toward the North Star. Estimate the distance between the two "pointer stars" and follow an imaginary line out for seven times that distance. There lies the North Star.

Because the north end of the earth's axis points toward the North Star, all the other stars and constellations appear to revolve around the North Star, while it alone stays still. This gave the star great magical importance to ancient peoples. (The real reason, of course, is the earth's rotation.) The Hindus called it the Pivot of the Planets. When Thuban was the North Star, it was so important to the Egyptians that they used it to line up the huge pyramids where their rulers were buried. The Great Pyramid of Cheops has a slanting central shaft 300 feet deep that once was aimed directly at Thuban. Every night of the year the star was visible from a chamber at the bottom of the shaft—until Thuban slipped away from its polar position.

Nova

In 1572 the great Danish astronomer Tycho Brahe coined a new term, *nova*. It was short for *nova stella*, the Latin for "new star," and it described a kind of star that flared up brightly where no star had been seen before, only to fade away afterward. It was thought that the nova was the birth of a new star. Not until the twentieth century did astronomers learn that novas were not new stars being born but old ones flaring up in a last burst of energy before they died. (It took so long to make this discovery because astronomers needed special instruments to analyze the light given off by stars.)

Novas are actually caused by eruptions in which a star belches out a large cloud of superhot, brightly-glowing gas. As the gas cools and drifts away, the light fades. Most novas and supernovas reach their greatest brightness in about two days. After that they remain bright for a year or so as they gradually fade away.

Some novas flare up several times. Most, however, either

disappear after the first flare-up or remain very faint. The brightest novas may give off 50,000 times as much light as our sun at their peak. But most novas cannot be seen without a telescope, for clouds of gas and dust in space screen out their light rays.

A special and very rare kind of nova is the *supernova*, which occurs perhaps once every 400 years in each galaxy, on the average. Ordinary novas appear to occur in ordinary-sized stars, and the stars are not destroyed by the flare-up. But supernovas take place only in giant stars. And the explosions are so violent that they blow the stars apart.

Astronomers theorize that as a giant star ages, eventually the nuclear fuel in its core is burned out. There is not enough energy left to support the vast outer layers of the star against the star's own gravity. The exhausted star then collapses in on itself, releasing a huge burst of energy with a flash that equals the brightness of millions of stars. What is left afterward is a very dense, small, faint core star, surrounded by a vast cloud of swirling gas.

The last supernova in our galaxy occurred in the constellation Taurus, in 1604. This supernova must have been unusually bright, for it terrified the astronomers of China. The Chinese loved law and order, and this nova must have seemed to them like a terrorist's bomb going off in heaven. Today this region is occupied by the famous Crab Nebula, with a small, dense, faint blue star in its center.

Ophiuchus

Ophiuchus is a constellation that is not in the zodiac and has no specially bright stars, but it is included in this book because of its odd name, which sounds like some obscure and long-extinct dinosaur. Actually Ophiuchus is Greek for "serpent-holder" (from *ophis*, "snake," and *echos*, "holder"), and thereby hangs a tail—a serpent's tail, that is, because Ophiuchus holds the writhing, snaky constellation Serpens.

The constellation was known as early as 1200 B.C. In the Middle East it was related to the sun-god Marduk's battle with the evil female sea-serpent Tiamat. But to the Greeks it was Asklepios, the god of medicine, better known to us under his Latin name of Aesculapius.

Aesculapius did not start life as a god, though he was one of the sons of Apollo. But he studied medicine under the centaur Chiron and became the world's first doctor. It is said that one day a big snake crawled into Aesculapius' room. Afraid of the reptile, he killed it and went about his business. But soon he noticed that another snake had come into the room, bearing a strange herb in its mouth. As he watched, the snake rubbed its dead mate with the herb and restored it to life. Aesculapius saw in a flash that here was the secret of immortality, and he seized the herb from the surprised serpent's jaws. He used it with great success to restore a number of dead Greek heroes to life. But Hades, Lord of the Underworld, complained to Zeus that these clever tricks of Aesculapius could end in his losing all his subjects in the Kingdom of the Dead. So when Aesculapius volunteered to restore the dead Orion to life, Zeus destroyed Aesculapius with a powerful thunderbolt. But Zeus later recognized Aesculapius' achievements in medical research by placing him in the sky together with a snake, which by this time had become his symbol.

The early Greeks thought that snakes had a special link to the gods. They were dreaded because many snakes are poisonous. But at the same time, they were thought to hold the secret of life, just as they held the secret of death.

Aesculapius was said to have served in the Trojan War. Long after this, the Greeks began to worship him as a god of medicine with a shrine at Epidaurus and others all over Greece, usually near a mineral spring or on a high mountain. Sick people would visit these shrines, and the god was supposed to visit them in their sleep and prescribe a remedy in their dreams.

There is a legend that once when Rome was suffering from a terrible plague, the Romans sent ambassadors to Epidaurus to ask Aesculapius to come and be their god of medicine, too.

117

The god answered in a dream, saying that he would appear the next day as a snake. The ambassadors took the snake with them on the next ship back to Rome. As the ship rowed up the Tiber River and neared the city's waterfront, the snake slipped overboard and swam to an island in the middle of the river. There a shrine and hospital were set up. Many modern Americans wish their doctors were as obliging about making house calls.

Orion

Orion, the Hunter, is the brightest constellation of the winter sky and one of the easiest to pick out as he stands with his uplifted club in one hand, feet widespread, and his starry belt marking his waist. Orion is one of the few constellations that looks at all like what it is supposed to represent, and it really does bear a resemblance to a human figure. In the ancient mythologies of different peoples it is always a supernatural hunter or giant, usually punished for wickedness or arrogance.

In Jewish tradition, Orion was Nimrod, Mighty Hunter before the Lord. At first a virtuous man, he was favored by God, who made him a powerful king. But Nimrod grew proud and arrogant and decided that he was the equal of God. He built the famous Tower of Babel, hoping to reach up to Heaven with it. God put a stop to this insolence by making the workmen unable to understand each other. Nimrod did not take the warning. Later, when a prophet told him that a child

119

would be born who would overthrow him, Nimrod sent his army out to kill seventy thousand innocent children. Finally God ended Nimrod's life and punished him by hanging him in the sky, where his soul could never find rest.

In Hindu mythology, Orion was a very strong but wicked giant named Prajapati, who had created man and the whole universe. He was slain just in time to prevent him from committing a monstrous sin. The story is told under SIRIUS.

In very old Egyptian myths Orion was the cannibal god Sahu, a fearsome being who stalked the skies, hunting down the other gods and feasting on their flesh. Sometimes he preyed on men, which hints at human sacrifice to this star-god.

The Sumerians, whose civilization was even older than that of Egypt, worshiped Orion as a Sun-God. They called him Uru-Anna, "Light of Heaven." Orion's name may possibly go back to this beginning, or it may come from a very old Greek name meaning "man of the mountain."

By far the best-known myths about Orion are Greek, and there are many variations on them. In one of them, Orion was the son of Poseidon, the Sea-God, and a nymph named Euryale. He grew up to be the handsomest man in the world, with a giant's strength. He traveled far and wide, hunting animals and fighting with heroes. He fell in love with a girl named Merope, whose father, Oenopion, was the king of an island infested with lions, wolves, and bears.

Oenopion (whose name means "Wine-a-plenty") promised Merope to Orion if the mighty hunter would get rid of all the wild beasts of prey. Orion accomplished this task quickly and flung the animals' skins at Oenopion's feet as proof. But Oenopion did not want to give up his daughter. Instead, he made Orion drunk. While the hunter lay unconscious, Oenopion put out his eyes and flung him onto the beach outside his palace gates.

With the help of the gods Orion got his sight back. Once more in good form, he boasted that he would rid the whole earth of wild beasts and monsters. He and Artemis, goddess of the moon and of hunting, fell in love. Apollo, her brother, did not like this at all. He resented the idea that his highborn sister might marry this boastful half-god, and he tricked Artemis into sending an arrow through Orion's head. Unable to restore him to life, she put his image among the stars.

Another legend tells how Orion's boasting made all the gods angry; so they persuaded the Earth-Goddess to send a little scorpion to sting Orion in the heel. The scorpion's venom proved fatal, and the mighty slayer of lions and bears was brought low by a crawling, despised vermin. Orion was placed in the skies, where the Scorpion constantly pursues him. This legend is an attempt to explain why Orion disappears for a part of the year when the constellation Scorpio rises above the horizon.

Myth aside, Orion is fascinating to astronomers because of its unusual number of bright stars, including Betelgeuse and Rigel. It also has the famed Great Nebula and the dark Horsehead Nebula, and more than seventy double stars.

Orion is accompanied in the skies by the constellations Canis Major ("Bigger Dog") and Canis Minor ("Smaller Dog"), natural companions for a hunter. The three stars of his belt point toward the bright star Sirius in Canis Major.

Perseus & Pegasus

Perseus is named for the Greek hero Perseus, who was the son of Zeus and a mortal woman named Danae. Perseus' grandfather, a king named Acrisius, had been told by an oracle that his grandson would kill him. So when Perseus was born, Acrisius locked the baby and his mother in a wooden chest and had them dumped into the sea, hoping they would drown and let him escape his fate. But the chest floated off to an island, and Danae and Perseus were rescued. Perseus grew up as the foster child of the king, Polydectes, whose name means "much welcoming."

Unfortunately Polydectes wanted to marry Danae, but she would not have him. This caused a good deal of trouble between Perseus and his foster father. Polydectes pretended that he was going to court another princess, however, and asked all his subjects to contribute a horse apiece to the bride-price he was going to offer the princess' father. (In those days a husband had to buy his wife from her parents. The idea was that he was taking a worker out of the family and should offer compensation.) Perseus had no horse to give, so he offered to get the head of the gorgon Medusa.

Medusa had once been a young, beautiful girl and a priestess of Athene. She had the bad luck to attract the attention of Poseidon, who raped her in Athene's temple. Athene was furious at the sacrilege. But instead of punishing Poseidon, who was one of the most powerful gods, she took her anger out on the innocent victim. She turned Medusa into a frightful monster with snakes for hair, huge teeth like a beast of prey, a tongue that lolled disgustingly out of her mouth, and a face that was so fearfully ugly that anyone who looked at it was turned to stone. For good measure, she did the same to Medusa's two sisters, who hadn't even been near when Poseidon committed his crime.

It was a rash vow that Perseus had made, and he regretted it as soon as he realized what he had said. However, Athene had overheard him. Still eager to punish Medusa, she helped Perseus with advice on gorgon-hunting. She warned him that he must on no account look Medusa directly in the face, or he would be turned to stone. She gave him a brightly polished shield to use as a mirror to see Medusa in. Not seeing her directly, he would not be turned to stone. From Hermes he got a magic sickle to cut off the gorgon's head. From the Stygian Nymphs he procured a pair of winged sandals with which he could fly through the air, a leather bag to hold the head, and the helmet of invisibility that belonged to Hades (Pluto).

With all this equipment, Perseus easily cut off Medusa's head while she slept. Her sisters, wakened by the noise, pursued Perseus, but he escaped by putting on the helmet of invisibility.

It was while he was on his way home to King Polydectes that he saw Andromeda chained to the rock and had his adventure with the monster Cetus. Afterward he delivered the gorgon's head as promised. He found that Polydectes was trying to marry Danae by force. So he whipped out the gorgon's head and turned Polydectes and all his supporters to stone. He then gave the head to Athene, who mounted it on her shield.

The constellation Perseus contains the famous star Algol, which the Greeks said was Medusa's head. It also contains a belt of meteoroids. When earth passes through this belt in August, spectacular meteor showers can be seen.

Pegasus, the winged horse of Greek mythology, is best known for his adventures with Bellerophon, the young hero who killed the monstrous Chimera. But he does have a connection with Perseus, for he was born full-grown from Medusa's corpse when Perseus had cut off her head. Some stories say that Poseidon created the winged horse from drops of Medusa's blood mixed with sand from the beach and sea foam.

The newborn Pegasus flew off to Mount Helicon, where he spent most of his time. Stamping his hoof on the ground, he opened up a spring called Hippocrene (Greek for "horse fountain.") Anyone who drank from this magic spring became a poet. On the strength of this legend, Pegasus became a symbol of artistic inspiration.

Bellerophon was a young man who had fled his home city in disgrace after killing his own brother. He sought refuge at the court of King Proetus, the uncle of Andromeda. But the king unjustly suspected Bellerophon of carrying on a love affair with his wife. The king sent Bellerophon to his royal father-in-law with a note requesting that the young man be quietly put out of the way. The king's father-in-law felt that it would be bad manners to kill his guest outright, so instead,

124

he sent Bellerophon to kill the Chimera. This was a female monster with the head of a lion, the body of a goat, and the tail of a serpent. Not only did she have dangerous teeth and claws, she also breathed fire. The king's father-in-law fully expected Bellerophon to be burned to a crisp and eaten by the Chimera. But once more Athene took a hand in things. She gave Bellerophon a golden bridle and told him to slip it over the head of Pegasus. When he had done this, the wild winged horse became tame.

Mounted on Pegasus, Bellerophon hovered safely out of range of the Chimera's fiery breath while he shot her full of arrows. Afterward Pegasus helped Bellerophon in other conquests, and the two became devoted to each other. But one day Bellerophon was overcome by pride—the worst thing that can happen to an ancient Greek hero—and persuaded Pegasus to carry him up to Olympus, for he thought he was as good as any of the gods. Zeus, infuriated, sent a fly to sting Pegasus. In pain and surprise, the winged horse bucked, and Bellerophon lost his grip and fell to earth, landing in a thorn bush. Lame and blinded, poor Bellerophon lived out the rest of his life as a lone, wandering beggar. Pegasus, for his part in the offense, was sentenced to the sky, where Zeus used him as a packhorse to carry his thunderbolts.

The constellation Pegasus, as pictured by the Greeks, shows half a winged horse, with his hindquarters missing. It is generally upside down in the sky, which makes it harder still to recognize. But Pegasus has an outstanding feature, the Great Square of Pegasus, which is easily seen with the naked eye. One corner of the square is the star that marks Andromeda's "head." The Great Square can be used in navigation when the Big Dipper is covered by clouds.

Pisces

Pisces is the twelfth and last constellation in the zodiac. Its name is Latin for "Fishes," and it is traditionally pictured as a pair of fishes with their tails loosely tied together by a long cord or ribbon. One swims east while the other is headed northeast by north.

Pisces is not the easiest constellation to find, for its stars are faint. It looks like a wide, straggly V, and not like a fish. But it is one of the ancient rainy-season constellations of the Middle East, and it lies in the part of the sky known as "The Sea." So "The Fishes" must have seemed like a logical name for it. The name is quite old, for it goes back at least to the Babylonians, who called the constellation *Nunu* ("fishes" in their language). The ancient Jews called it *Dagaim* and considered it their national constellation. This is rather strange, because Pisces was also closely identified with the pagan fish-god Dagon, national deity of the Philistines, who were the bitter enemies of the Jews.

The Greek myth of the origin of Pisces goes back to the same swimming party of the Gods at which Aries and Capricorn originated. When the monster Typhon appeared Aphrodite and her son Eros dashed for the water and turned into fishes. As mother and son, they are linked in the stars.

As a water constellation, Pisces was credited with power over sailors. But it was not the sailor's friend. It was feared as a cause of storms and shipwrecks (probably because it coincided with the stormy season of March). In fact, many peoples regarded Pisces as unlucky. The Egyptians supposedly would not eat sea fish because they were Pisces creatures and bearers of misfortune. The Chinese, who called the stars of Pisces the Eight Chiefs, considered the constellation a great source of evil. In the Chinese zodiac, Pisces was the Sign of the Pig. The Mongols called Pisces the Eight Devils and believed that it protected robbers.

In astrology, Pisces sumbolizes the Great Flood and the end of the sun's journey through the zodiac. Some astrologers hold that it also represents mental indifference. When other people take things seriously, Pisceans shrug their shoulders and let them pass. Pisceans are said to be charming and magnetic, or else shy. Both sorts are said to have vivid, romantic imaginations. Its lucky gem is the bloodstone; the lucky day is Friday, the lucky numbers are five and eight; the lucky color is lavender (some astrologers say blue and green). Not surprisingly, Pisceans are supposed to succeed best at the seashore or in cities near the sea.

Planet

Night after night, ancient Greek herdsmen and temple priests, scanning the skies, noticed that certain bright heavenly bodies were continually moving about, while the others either seemed to stand still or moved very, very slowly around the sky. These fast-moving bodies they named *planetai*, or "wanderers." Today we call them *planets*.

The ancient Greeks counted seven heavenly bodies as planets: Mercury, Venus, Mars, Jupiter, and Saturn, plus the moon and sun. The last two were added because the Greeks, like most ancient peoples, believed that the earth was the center of the universe, and that the sun revolved around it. For the same reason, they didn't recognize that earth itself is a planet. The moon, of course, actually does orbit the earth, although today it ranks as a satellite rather than a planet.

Today we count as planets only those heavenly bodies that orbit the sun. There are nine of them: starting with the one nearest the sun they are Mercury, Venus, earth, Mars, Jupiter,

Saturn, Uranus, Neptune, and Pluto. Except for earth, all of them are named for various Greek or Roman gods, though the three outer planets, too far away to see with the naked eye, were not discovered until relatively recent times. Uranus was not discovered until 1781, Neptune in 1846, and Pluto in 1930. But the Greeks had already set the pattern of naming the planets after gods with whom they were associated.

The Greeks—and all other ancient civilizations—believed that the planets controlled human affairs, or at least had a very strong influence. They endowed them with all sorts of pseudohuman qualities, even with a sort of watchful intelligence. These superstitious beliefs were taken very seriously. Even today many astrology fans claim to believe the same things. This is fun for astrology buffs, of course, but as yet there is no scientific proof that the planets or stars have any effect on what humans think, feel, or do.

One theory holds that the planets were formed from great masses of incandescent gas that were spewed out of the sun. As this glowing-hot gas cooled, it condensed into gigantic "droplets" that fell into orbit around the sun. A more modern theory is that the sun and planets were formed at the same time from a great cloud of cosmic dust. This is the Nebular Hypothesis, which you can read about under NEBULA. Whichever theory is true, the planets are all quite different in size, distance from the sun, and conditions on their surface.

The four planets nearest to the sun—Mercury, Venus, earth, and Mars, are heavy for their size. They are composed mainly of metal and rock. Jupiter and the outer planets are lightweights, composed mainly of frozen gases surrounding a small core of rock or metal.

The planets travel around the sun in elliptical paths—that is, paths shaped like a flattened-out circle. Furthermore, their orbits are all more or less eccentric, that is, off-center; so at some points in their orbits they are much closer to the sun than at others.

Are there other solar systems in the universe, other planets orbiting other stars? With all the billions of stars that exist, the chances are very good that there are many other solar systems. But they are so far away from earth that even traveling at the speed of light it would take almost a lifetime to reach even the nearest of them. Sending radio messages to intelligent beings in other solar systems—if there are any—would take just as long. So we may never know whether or not there is other life in the universe.

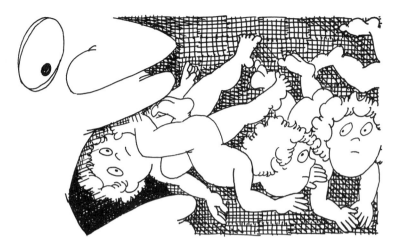

Pluto

Pluto, the planet farthest from the sun, is named for the Greco-Roman God of the Underworld, the pitiless Ruler of the Dead. Originally Pluto's name was Hades, which may mean "The Unseen One," but the Greeks so feared this god that they were afraid to mention him by name. Instead they called him by flattering titles like "The Giver of Good Counsel" and "The Receiver of Many" (that is, many dead souls).

Hades was one of the children of Cronus the Titan, a most unpleasant creature who had castrated and murdered his own father, Uranus, and ruled the world in his stead. Cronus then took the precaution of swallowing each of his own children as soon as they were born to prevent them from treating him the same way. Only one—Zeus—escaped. Zeus later tricked Cronus into vomiting up his brothers and sisters, and the young gods and goddesses made war on their wicked father and the other Titans.

After a ten-year struggle they defeated him and divided up the spoils. To Zeus fell the heavens, to Poseidon the sea, and to Hades the underworld, with all the gems and precious metals hidden beneath the earth.

Hades' kingdom was a dark, cold, gloomy place, which he ruled like the warden of a maximum-security prison. Forbidden to return to earth, the wretched ghosts of the dead flitted about aimlessly, twittering like bats. It is no wonder that the Greeks dreaded Hades. Later, however, their ideas about him changed, and the god became kindlier. He also got a new name, *Ploutos*, "The Wealthy One." The Romans changed this name slightly to *Pluto* to make it sound more Roman—they didn't like to mouth names invented by a lot of jabbering foreigners. In fact, they preferred to call him Dis Pater, "Wealthy Father." But Pluto is the name by which this ancient deity is best known today.

The planet Pluto is so small, so faint, and so distant from earth that it is extremely hard to observe. It takes a twelve-inch telescope to pick it up, and then you must know in just what part of the sky to look. Astronomers believe that Pluto is probably about 3,700 miles (6,000 kilometers) in diameter—less than half the size of earth—making it the second smallest of all the planets. Pluto probably has a very rough surface, since it reflects so little light.

Pluto has the most eccentric orbit of all the planets, traveling between 2,800 million and 4,600 million miles (4,425–7,375 million kilometers) from the sun. During part of its orbit it is actually closer to the sun than Neptune is. Time would pass very slowly for an earthman on Pluto. The planet takes 247.7 years to complete a single orbit of the sun, and from sunrise to sunrise is nearly a week. It is impossible to measure the temperature on this distant chunk of matter, but astronomers have estimated it at anywhere from −290° to −380° F (−179° to −229° C)—close to absolute zero.

Because Pluto is so small and so distant, it was not discovered until 1930. Its existence was suspected by two leading American astronomers, Percival Lowell and William Pickering. Astronomers had noticed tiny irregularities in the orbits of Uranus and Neptune. Lowell and Pickering believed that the cause of these deviations must be another planet in orbit beyond them. After years of observations and intricate calculations, Lowell worked out the probable orbit of his suspected planet in 1915. Lowell died in 1916, but other men carried on his search as part of the work at the great observatory which Lowell had founded at Flagstaff, Arizona. Year after year, staff astronomers pored over photographic plates, searching for some hint of a moving body that would be the sought-after planet. At last, in January 1930, a young astronomer named Clyde Tombaugh noticed a faint speck of light that seemed to have shifted its position from photograph to photograph. It was, indeed, Lowell's unknown planet, only 5 degrees from where he had predicted it would be found. Ironically, modern astronomers think Lowell's calculations were off the mark. The mass of Pluto is too small to influence its neighbor planets as he thought it did. Still, it was Lowell's calculations, right or wrong, that led to Pluto's discovery. Cold, dark, and unreachable by living men, it is fittingly named after the ancient Greek Lord of the Underworld.

Quasar

Quasars are one of the great mysteries of astronomy. Their existence was not even suspected until the early 1960s, and scientists are still not certain of what they actually are or where they came from. All that we know is that quasars look like stars, are probably a few times bigger than our solar system, and give off huge amounts of radio energy. They are also extremely bright in proportion to their size.

After World War II, radio astronomers began to discover many objects in space that gave off radio waves but no visible light waves. Eventually these radio sources were tracked down, and some were found to be nebulas. Others were distant galaxies or the remains of exploding supernovas. But in 1960 two astronomers trained a radio telescope on what seemed to be a faint star. They picked up an intense burst of radio-wave radiation. Astronomers all over the world were astonished by this discovery, but soon a number of similar starlike objects were found. The scientists named them quasars, short for quasi-stellar radio sources. Quasi is Latin for "as if," "just like," or "seemingly." Stellar (from stella, "star") is Latin for "starlike" or "of a star." And quasars did appear to be like stars in some ways but they certainly behaved in a most unstarlike manner.

For one thing, they periodically flared up and dimmed much faster than any ordinary star. Though small, they gave off as much light as a hundred good-sized galaxies averaging 100 billion stars each. Then there is their radio energy. Actually all stars give off radio waves, but a single quasar may give off as much radio energy as a million Milky Ways.

Quasars are faint, despite all their energy, because they are so far from earth. But if it had not been for the sound of a train whistle more than a hundred years ago, scientists might still be without a way to measure such vast interstellar distances. About 1840, an Austrian physicist, Christian Doppler, became intrigued by the fact that a train's whistle seemed to slide up to a higher pitch as the train chuffed off into the distance. Doppler reasoned that the sound waves behaved as if they got shorter (thus rising in pitch) as the train approached and longer (thus producing a lower pitch) as the train departed. He reasoned that the sound waves of the whistle reached him at an increasing frequency as the train approached and at a decreasing frequency as the train drew away. This discovery was called the "Doppler effect."

Twentieth-century astronomers discovered that the Doppler effect works for light waves as well as for sound waves. Light from an approaching star gets shifted toward the violet end of the spectrum as its waves are "shortened" by the Doppler effect. Light from a star moving away from the observer shifts toward the red end of the spectrum as its waves are "lengthened." The greater the distance of the star and the greater the speed at which it is moving away from earth, the greater the "red shift" is. By analyzing the light waves of quasars, astronomers calculated that the quasars are moving away from earth at almost the speed of light and that they are almost unbelievably distant from the solar system. The farthest known quasar is estimated to be 10 billion light-years away!

Now, light travels at 186,000 miles per second, and in a year it travels about 6 trillion miles. So, written out with all its zeros, the distance of this quasar would be 60,000,000,000,-000,000,000,000 miles from earth, and it is getting farther away even as you read this sentence.

Of course, such great numbers are more than anyone can really imagine except as a string of zeros on a piece of paper. But quasars can have practical uses. Right now, NASA scientists are using them to help predict earthquakes. In California there is a fault zone—a weak place in the earth's crust— where very severe earthquakes have taken place. The scientists set up radio telescopes on each side of the fault. Then they used radio waves from a quasar to measure the distance between the telescopes very accurately. Because the radio telescopes are many miles apart, the radio waves reach one a fraction of a second before they reach the other. If this time interval changes, the scientists know that the earth's crust has moved, changing the distance between the two telescopes. Monitoring the shifts in the earth's crust, in turn, may help other scientists predict when an earthquake is likely to occur.

Rigel

Rigel, which marks the left foot of Orion, is the seventh-brightest star visible from earth, giving off 40,000 times as much light as the sun. Its name comes from the Arabic *Rijl Jauza al-Yusrah*, meaning "Left Foot of the Central One." Another Arabic name for this blue-white giant star was *Ra'i al-Jauzah*, "Herdsman of the Central One." The Arabs thought of the other stars in the constellation as a herd of camels. Rigel, the brightest, was supposed to be the herdsman.

In Norse mythology, Rigel was the big toe of a mighty giant named Orvandil who was rash enough to fight Thor, the Thunder God. Orvandil was an ice giant, one of a breed that threatened to take over the whole world and turn it into a frozen wasteland. Since this would have left the gods without any worshipers, they were constantly battling the ice giants to thwart their plans for conquest. When Orvandil fought Thor, the Thunder God overcame him after a titanic struggle (fighting was something the Norsemen loved to hear about

137

and worked it into all their stories). One of Orvandil's big toes was frozen so hard that Thor broke it clean off and hurled it up among the stars of the Great Bear. The rest of the frozen giant Thor placed in the sky, much as a modern "sportsman" would hang the stuffed head of a moose on his wall. Thor's trophy was the same constellation we call Orion.

Rigel is a double star, but one of the pair is much smaller than the other—so small that it is almost invisible even with a telescope. Astrologers say that it is a lucky star to be born under, probably because its brightness seemed like a favorable sign to the ancient skywatchers.

Sagittarius

Sagittarius, the ninth sign of the zodiac, represents the centaur Chiron, a prominent character in Greek mythology. The centaurs were a strange race of beings, human down to the waist and horse below, complete with four feet and swishing tail. The Greeks may have gotten the original idea for the centaurs from long-gone fights with some tribe of horsemen, who rode so skillfully that they almost seemed half man and half horse. Or the original centaurs may have been some wild, rough clan of mountain-dwellers with the horse as their totem. At any rate, in the Greek tales the centaurs are wild and savage, live in the mountains, and are almost always at war with one or more clans of Greeks.

There was one centaur who was not at all savage. In fact he was one of the most civilized beings in all the Greek myths. This was Chiron, the king of the centaurs. Chiron, whose name means "Handy," was one of the wisest beings on earth. He was skilled in medicine and could prophesy the future. He taught Jason, Achilles, Hercules, and other famous heroes. Supposedly Chiron was the first to arrange the stars in constellations, so that men could use them to tell directions and to foresee the changing of the seasons. With pardonable pride he outlined one figure of the zodiac in his own image.

Some time after this, Hercules accidentally wounded his old teacher Chiron with a poisoned arrow. The poison was magical, so that even Chiron's medicines could not counteract it. The poor centaur was in agony. But he could not escape his pain by dying, for he was immortal. At last Zeus took pity on him and let him die, but preserved his image in the stars.

Sagittarius is pictured as a rearing centaur armed with a bow and arrow pointed straight at the heart of the Scorpion. This is how the constellation got its name, which is Latin for "archer." Like the other constellations of the zodiac, Sagittarius dates back to the early Sumerian and Babylonian astronomers. The peoples of the Middle East were very fond of imagining creatures that were fantastic mixtures of man and beast, and Sagittarius may originally have been Enkidu, a Sumerian hero who was half man and half bull. Incidentally, the Greeks sometimes called Sagittarius "the Bull-killer" because when Sagittarius rises in the east, the stars of Taurus sink out of sight in the west.

The constellation Sagittarius has no very bright stars, but it does have two interesting star-groups called the Milk Dipper and the Southern Crown.

In astrology, Sagittarius is ruled by Jupiter and represents authority and physical power. The lucky day is Thursday, the lucky gem is the turquoise, the lucky number is nine, and the lucky color is purple. Sagittarians are supposed to be honest, happy-go-lucky, clumsy, and tactless, but with a great ability to make and keep friends in spite of often putting their feet in their mouths.

Some say that Sagittarius is not really Chiron, but another centaur named Crotus. According to this theory, Chiron is the constellation Centaurus, which lies much further south in the sky. This constellation contains the bright yellow star Proxima Centauri.

Satellite

Satellite comes from the Latin *satelles*, meaning "attendant" or "guard." In French this became *satellite*, and in this form it marched into the English language in the fifteen hundreds. By the middle sixteen hundreds astronomers had discovered that several of the planets had smaller heavenly bodies circling around them like dutiful attendants around their masters. And so these planetary "attendants" were named satellites. Another name for them is "moons."

In all, there are 34 known satellites in the solar system. Jupiter has four large moons and ten small ones. Saturn has ten moons. Neptune has two, Uranus five, and Mars two. Venus, Mercury, and Pluto have none, as far as is known. Earth, of course, has the moon.

Titan, one of the moons of Saturn, is the largest satellite in the solar system, with an estimated diameter of 3,600 miles (5,800 kilometers). Two of Jupiter's moons, Ganymede and Callisto, are close runners-up. The smallest is the fourteenth moon of Jupiter, which is only four miles across.

Titan is the only satellite that has an atmosphere. We know this because when we watch through a telescope as Titan begins to cross in front of a star, the tiny point of light that is the star becomes blurred just before it disappears behind the satellite. With any other satellite, the star remains clear. This is how astronomers knew the moon had no atmosphere hundreds of years before any space probe landed there.

Small as the satellites are in relation to their planets, they do have some influence on them. The satellite's gravity tugs on the planet just as the planet's does on the satellite. So while the satellite is orbiting around the planet, the planet and satellite together orbit around a common center. It is something like a big ice skater and a small skater with both hands linked together, swinging around in circles as they glide along the ice.

The telescope has showed us the mountains and craters of the moon, and photos taken in space revealed that the moons of Mars are rough and pockmarked. But nothing is known of the surface details of the satellites of Jupiter and the planets that lie beyond.

The first man-made satellite was launched into orbit in 1957. It was a small Russian craft named Sputnik (Russian for "companion") that circled the earth for months, beeping out radio signals. In many countries, people consulted their newspapers to see when Sputnik would pass overhead. They would rush out to see the little metal globe scoot by in the night sky like a very fast-moving star.

Sputnik came as a terrible shock to Americans. We had long prided ourselves on being the technological leaders of the world—and here were the "backward" Russians beating us into space. Determined not to be outdone, the United States pushed its own space program ahead frantically. The two nations engaged in a space race that lasted over 10 years. The Russians kept a narrow lead in many achievements, such as getting the first man into orbit and landing the first unmanned spacecraft on the moon. But the United States won the crowning victory by landing the first men on the moon, and getting them back alive and in good health.

Much has been learned about space from the manned and unmanned spacecraft. In orbit beyond earth's atmosphere, astronauts can see and photograph the stars and planets with much greater clarity. Samples of rock and dust brought back from the moon by American astronauts are already giving clues to the origins of the solar system. But smaller satellites perform valuable jobs every day. Communication satellites relay telephone conversations, news, and TV programs over the widest oceans. Weather satellites beam back photos of weather patterns so that meteorologists can forecast storms. Other earth-observing satellites help oceanographers by picking out the patterns of ocean currents. Still others monitor growing crops. The list of uses is almost endless.

Saturn

Saturn, the sixth planet from the sun, is named for a Roman god of agriculture, Saturnus. Saturnus was a very ancient god of sowing and harvesting, and he was worshiped in Italy for centuries before Rome began. The Romans were farmers, too, in the early days, and they worshiped Saturnus in the hope of getting good crops.

Saturnus—or Saturn, to use his modern name—was thought to have lived on earth as a king before he became a god, ruling over a golden age of peace, plenty, and contentment. His emblem was a sickle, the tool with which men and women harvested grain (scythes had not yet been invented). Later on, the Romans identified this ancient harvest deity with the Greek god Cronus (the father of Zeus and the other gods of Olympus). By a further mix-up, they confused him with Chronos, the spirit of Time. Our cartoon figure of Father Time, with scythe and hourglass, is really Saturn in disguise.

In addition to being a harvest god, Saturn also became a god of the year's end. Each year the Romans held a festival in his honor on December 17. The celebration, called *Saturnalia*, was like a combination of Christmas, New year's Eve, and a rock festival. People exchanged gifts; masters waited hand and foot on their slaves; and everybody feasted, drank, and carried on in ways that they would normally never dare to.

Saturn also ruled the last day of the week. The Romans called it *Saturni dies* ("Saturn's day"). The Anglo-Saxons turned it into *Sacternes daeg*. Today we call it Saturday.

Saturn was the furthest planet known to the ancients, as it is the furthest that can be seen with the naked eye. Of course, Babylonians, Egyptians, Greeks, and Romans didn't know how far it was from earth. To them it was a bright, unwinking, star trekking around a regular path in the heavens. In the Near East, Saturn was considered to be the planet of the Hebrews—each people had its own patron planet or star that watched over them.

Stripped of its mythology, Saturn is a giant globe about 76,000 miles (120,000 kilometers) in diameter. The second largest of the planets, it is composed mainly of hydrogen and helium, with a small core of rock and metal. Astronomers have calculated that it is lighter than water and would float if only a large enough tub could be found to place it in. That is, it would float if it didn't freeze the water first, for Saturn's temperature has been measured at about $-290°$ F $(-180°$ C).

Saturn has ten moons, but it is best known for the mysterious bright rings that circle it. The rings are thought to be composed of small rock particles about the size of coarse sand, or possibly small ice crystals of the same size. They may have been formed by one or more moons breaking up. Saturn has three rings (the inner-most is visible only through the most powerful telescopes). The rings are huge. The outer ring, for example, measures about 172,400 miles (277,600 kilometers) from edge to edge, and it is about 11,000 miles (17,700 kilometers) broad. Astronomers estimate the thickness of the rings anywhere from 100 miles (161 kilometers) down to a few inches.

As Saturn tilts in its orbit, the position of the rings as seen from earth changes. They appear to increase or shrink in width as the angle changes. When they are edge-on they are practically invisible.

The rings were first seen by the great Italian scientist Galileo—the first person to use a telescope in astronomy—in 1610. However, Galileo was never able to get a second look at them, owing to changes in their position, and he was never sure that they were not an illusion. They were not proven real until 1855, nearly two and a half centuries later.

In ancient medicine, Saturn was believed to cause people to be sluggish, cold-natured, and gloomy. From this comes the expression "saturnine temperament." Since the development of modern psychology, other words are used to describe this type of personality, but "saturnine" is still in the dictionary.

In astrology, Saturn rules the sign of Capricorn. When favorable, it gives steadfastness, justice, and vitality. When unfavorable, it causes hypocrisy, discontent, and greed. The mystical metal of Saturn is lead, which may be why astrological guides say that Saturn is a good sign for dealing with plumbers.

Scorpio

Scorpio is the eighth constellation in the zodiac. Modern astronomers call it Scorpius. Both are Latin names for the scorpion, a venomous little animal that is a traditional symbol of harm.

Scorpions look rather like small lobsters, with their long tails and pincer claws. But they are more closely related to spiders. Scorpions carry a poisonous stinger in the tips of their tails, which they use to kill their prey and to defend themselves from larger animals that prey on them. Only a few kinds of scorpions are deadly to man, but all of them have a very painful sting, and most kinds can make a victim feel pretty sick. The scorpion's reputation can be judged by the fact that a specially painful whip for beating slaves and criminals was called a scorpion. It had several lashes, and each was tipped with a ball of lead or an iron spike. "Scorpion" was also the name of a kind of catapult for hurling medium-sized rocks at enemy armies.

Scorpions range from an inch (2.54 centimeters) or so in length to six inches (15.3 centimeters). They live in the warmer parts of the world, hiding from the sun's heat by day and coming out to hunt at night. They can be dangerous because they creep into bedding, shoes, and clothes left on the ground. When an unsuspecting human comes into contact with them, their instinct is to sting. Scorpions are very common in the Middle East, where our system of astronomy began.

The constellation Scorpius actually suggests the shape of a scorpion with its tail poised to sting (the animal curves its tail forward and darts it into its victim). The name can be traced back to the Sumerians, who called it *Girtab*, "The Stinger." The Hebrews and Arabs called it *Akrab*, "scorpion," and the Greeks called it *Skorpios*.

Scorpius was feared almost universally as a symbol of darkness and death. Not only are real scorpions creatures of darkness, but the sun enters the constellation at the season when the year is dying, and the nights are dark and long. Interestingly, the Mayas in Mexico and Central America, who had no contact with the civilizations of Europe or Asia, called it the "Sign of the Death-God."

Scorpius lies opposite Orion in the sky, and when Scorpius rises Orion sets. When Orion rises, Scorpius slinks below the horizon. To the ancients, it must have seemed like a never-ending battle. This probably gave rise to many legends like the Greek one that tells how the goddess Hera sent a scorpion to kill the hero Orion, for she was tired of listening to his boasts. The mighty hunter was brought low by a contemptible little creature that crawled on the ground! Hera was overjoyed—she was a spiteful lady—and triumphantly put the scorpion in the sky. In older legends, Orion was a sun-god, the friend of man. The Scorpion was the enemy who slew him.

Not all peoples considered Scorpius an evil constellation, however. The Chinese once pictured it as part of the kindly Blue Dragon of the East. Later it became the sign of the

Hare—certainly not a dangerous animal—in the Chinese zodiac.

The Polynesians, whose islands have no scorpions, have their own legends about Scorpius. The chief god was given a magic jawbone by his grandmother, who ruled the Land of the Dead. The god smeared some of his own blood—a powerful charm—on the jawbone and tied it to his fishhook, made from a carefully ground piece of pearl shell. No sooner had he thrown out his line than he felt the hook catch on something. He gave it a sharp tug, but it didn't move. He tugged harder and harder and finally hauled in his prize—an island, complete with trees, mountains, houses, people, and even barking dogs. His hook had sunk down through the ocean to the Kingdom of Night, on the other side of the world, and caught the island. Delighted with his catch, the god joyfully flung his fishhook up into the sky, where we now see it outlined in stars.

Astronomically, Scorpius is a very conspicuous constellation, with many beautiful stars. Its brightest star is the super-giant red star Antares, which marks the "heart" of the Scorpion.

In astrology, Scorpio signifies death, deceit (the ancients could never forgive the scorpion for having its sting in its tail instead of up front like snakes and spiders), and fruitfulness. It is ruled by Mars, the red planet that is often confused with Antares by skywatchers. Its lucky gem is the topaz; the lucky day is Tuesday; the lucky numbers are three and five; the lucky color is dark red.

Scorpio is also said to stand for the fall of man from his original purity, and for his final victory over sin. Scorpios are supposed to be full of ideas and suggestions, and to have great willpower and determination. They make dangerous enemies, but good friends. The author of this book is a Scorpio.

Sirius

Sirius, the "Dog Star," marks the nose of Canis Major, the Big Dog. Its name comes from the Greek *seirios*, meaning "sparkling" or "scorching." Both meanings are justified when it comes to Sirius, the first because of the star's brightness, the second because in ancient times the appearance of Sirius coincided with the hottest weather of the year. The Greeks also called it *Kyon*, "dog"; *Kyon Seirios*, "sparkling dog"; *Kyon Aster*, "dog star"; and simply *To Astron*, "the star."

In ancient Egypt Sirius was called the Star of the Nile because its appearance in the sky heralded the yearly rising of the great river, bringing water and rich silt to Egypt's riverside fields. The star's name in Egypt was Sihor, which may have suggested *seirios* to the Greeks.

Since very ancient times Sirius has been called a dog star. The reason may be that it once rose in the constellation Leo (the lion) in early July. The lion and the hunting dog are both fierce animals, and ancient peoples connected this fierceness with the fierce heat of the sun. From this coincidence came the expression "dog days," the hottest, most uncomfortable part of summer. Today, however, Sirius is a winter star.

Not all peoples of the ancient world thought of Sirius as a dog, however. The Hindus called it the Deerslayer and told this story about it. A wicked star-giant named Prajapati fell in love with his own daughter, the beautiful Red Deer, Rohini, whom we in the West know as the star Aldebaran. Changing himself into a stag, he pursued the horrified maiden around the sky. Just as he was overtaking her, Sirius, who was not a dog, but a hunter, came to her rescue. With a three-pointed arrow he dropped Prajapati in his tracks. The giant remained in the skies, with the three stars of the arrow sticking out of his side. In the West, the arrow is called Orion's Belt, for the wicked giant of India was Orion the Hunter.

Sirius is not only the brightest star in Canis Major but the brightest star visible from earth. It is brilliant white, although it seems to have been red in ancient times. The Romans used to sacrifice a red or fawn-colored dog to Sirius, matching its color, at the start of the dog days. They hoped in this way to put the star in a good mood so that it would not scorch and wither their crops.

Sirius has a white dwarf companion star which is only about three times the diameter of earth and has 250,000 times the mass of earth. An average-sized man would weigh 2,600 tons on Sirius' companion. However, he would be squashed flat by the immensely powerful gravity before he could even climb on the scales.

Sun

Sun is the star around which earth revolves, the center of our solar system. The sun's name comes from the Anglo-Saxon word *sunne*, which scholars trace back to a very old Indo-European root, *sun*, that may carry the idea of something shining. The Latin name for the Sun is *sol*, from which our adjective *solar* comes. The Greeks called the Sun *helios*, which was also one of their names for the sun-god. The gas *helium* bears its name because it was first discovered in the sun.

The sun is masculine in some languages and feminine in others. It was feminine in English until about 1500, so that people referred to the sun as "she." In German, it is still a "she," but in French and Spanish it is a "he."

This confusion over the sun's gender goes back to the times when man worshiped the sun. Sometimes people thought of the great fire in the sky as masculine, the husband of the moon; sometimes it was the other way around, with mother sun being the moon's wife. (Sometimes also they were father and son or mother and daughter.) But by either sex, the sun was one of the most important gods to early man. The sun gave warmth and life as well as light for men and women to see by. Its rays chased away the evil demons of the night and the real beasts of prey that hunted by night.

As mankind developed more elaborate religions, the sun sometimes lost importance. But in at least three religions it became the central figure. One was Mithraism, a Near Eastern religion that the Roman army took up with great enthusiasm. The central figure here was Mithra, who bears some resemblance to Jesus, and who was called *Sol Invictus*, "The Unconquered Sun," by his Roman worshipers.

In ancient Persia, the official religion was Zoroastrianism, named for the prophet who founded it. Zoroaster taught that two gods, the good Ahura-Mazda and the bad Ahriman, were perpetually struggling for control of the world. Ahura-Mazda's symbols were fire and the sun. The Persians worshiped Ahura-Mazda until Moslem invaders from Arabia stormed into their land and forced everyone to become a Moslem or suffer death. A few who clung to the old faith escaped to India, where they are known as Parsees ("Persians").

In the high Andes of South America, the Incas worshipped the sun above all other gods, of which they had many. The Inca himself, their sacred emperor, was supposed to be an incarnation of the sun. The sun-god's proper name was Viracocha, and the Incas claimed that he had created the first Inca man and woman, taught them everything they needed to know, and commanded them to rule all other peoples and teach them civilization.

One of the practical uses man made of the sun was in telling time. The sun marked the seasons, and also the time of day. A farmer knew that when the sun rose high over that hill beyond his field, it was midsummer. When the Sun rose off to the side of the hill, it was time to get ready for winter. A person might say to a friend, "Meet me when the sun is halfway up the sky." Later, man invented sundials to tell the time of day by the shadow the sun cast.

The fuss that people made over the sun in prescientific days was based mostly on ignorance and superstition. But they were correct in believing that the sun was important. For life as we know it could not exist without the sun. The sun's rays provide the warmth that living things need for their chemical processes to take place. Green plants trap the energy in the sun's light and turn it into sugars and starches. Plant-eating animals live on these foods created by plants from sunlight, and predators live on the plant-eaters, all the way up the great network of life.

The sun is also the main source of energy for man. Oil, coal, and gas are sunlight-energy stored up by plants millions of years ago. When these resources run low, we may rely more on wind power. The wind, too, is mainly caused by the sun, which heats the earth's air and sets up currents in it. And already scientists are using the Sun's rays directly to create electricity. So far solar power cells have been used only experimentally and on spacecraft, for they are still very inefficient and expensive. But it will probably not be too many more years before this clean, nonpolluting form of energy is much more widely used.

For all its importance to us, the sun is only a medium-sized star, in a universe filled with billions of stars. Of course, it is far bigger than our own planet. Its diameter is about 864,000 miles (1,400,000 kilometers), 109 times the diameter of earth. It contains an estimated 330,000 times as much matter as earth. In fact, it contains over ninety-eight percent of all the matter in the solar system. The temperature at the sun's core is believed to be between 25 million and 30 million degrees Fahrenheit (14 and 16.7 million degrees C). At the surface, it is 11,000° F. (6,100° C). The sun's surface is "cool" because it is constantly losing energy that radiates out into space. A portion of this energy is our sunlight.

The sun is composed mainly of hydrogen, and the energy that heats it to such fantastic temperatures comes from nuclear reactions that fuse hydrogen atoms into helium atoms. Each second an estimated 655,000,000 tons of hydrogen are converted into 650,000,000 tons of helium. The remaining 5,000,000 tons are converted into energy. In spite of the staggering amounts of matter that are used up so rapidly, the sun has probably been burning at the same rate for four or five billion years and will probably continue to burn at this rate for several billion more.

Observing the sun is difficult because of its brightness. Looking at the sun directly for even a few seconds is enough to blind you temporarily, and doctors say it may damage your eyes permanently. Anyone who looks at the Sun without proper eye protection through a magnifying glass, binoculars, or telescope will suffer severe eye damage instantly. Even looking through exposed film may be dangerous. Scientific observers use specially designed dark filters. DON'T TAKE ANY CHANCES!

The first person to make scientific observations of the sun was Galileo, in 1610, using the newly invented telescope and taking precautions to protect his vision. Galileo was the first person to see sunspots, and this got him into trouble with the

Roman Catholic Church. The Greek philosophers, whose ideas about astronomy the Church had adopted, taught that the sun was perfect. Now this impudent Galileo claimed that he had seen blemishes on its face. The men who ruled the Church took this as a challenge to their doctrines. They feared that if the Church were proven wrong on any point, it would be challenged on every point, and possibly lose its power. Eventually Galileo was punished for his reports of the sunspots and other astronomical sins.

Much has been learned about the sun since Galileo's time, thanks to improved telescopes and other instruments that allow us to analyze its light, measure its magnetism, and so on. Much more will be learned from orbiting space labs in the years to come. This knowledge will be valuable not only for its own sake but because it may help us to tap the sun's vast stores of energy for our own use.

Taurus

Taurus the Bull, the second constellation of the zodiac, is one of the constellations of spring. Its name is the Latin word for "bull," and it was probably named because a group of stars in the constellation look a bit like the head of a bull. Undoubtedly there was also religious symbolism at work, for Taurus was the constellation of the spring equinox from 4000 to 1700 B.C. The Sumerians and Babylonians thought of Taurus as the Bull of Heaven, who plowed the Furrow of Heaven that opened the new planting and growing season.

Cattle were important in the ancient Middle East. They furnished milk, cheese, and an occasional treat of meat. When they died or were slaughtered, their hides became leather. More important yet, they pulled plows and carts, sparing men's and women's tired muscles. The cow was an emblem of motherhood and fertility. The bull was a symbol of strength, ferocity, and male sexual power. Many peoples worshiped bull-gods. The Egyptians had a bull-god named Apis. On earth he was represented by a real bull, chosen by Apis' priests on the basis of his color and markings. The Apis-bull was kept in a magnificent stall in the temple and given every luxury a bull could want. When the Apis-bull died, his body was buried with honors in a special cemetery for the sacred bulls. If the bull were obstinate enough to live for twenty-five years, the priests did away with him and told the people that he had committed suicide. A splendid funeral and the search for a new Apis made the worshipers forget their grief soon enough.

When the Israelites were wandering in the desert after leaving Egypt, the Bible tells us, some of them made a golden calf and worshiped it. This was simply backsliding to the ways of their pagan ancestors, who had once worshiped a bull-god. The legend of the Minotaur probably preserves the memory of a nearly forgotten bull-god worshiped by the Cretans. To Hindus, cows and bulls are so sacred that it is considered a sin to kill one and a worse sin to eat its flesh. Hindus explain that eating beef is like eating your own mother.

Compared to all this, the Greek legend of Taurus sounds rather flippant. The insatiable Zeus fell in love with a mortal princess named Europa. But he knew that his suspicious wife Hera would be watching him. So he disguised himself in the form of a beautiful, snow-white bull with golden horns and materialized among the royal herd of cattle. Europa noticed the handsome, friendly beast who seemed to be begging for her attention. She soon treated him like a pet, scratching him between the horns and bringing him dainties from the royal table. One day she climbed on his back. The crafty Zeus immediately dashed into the sea and swam off to the far-away island of Crete, where he resumed his own shape and had an affair with the astonished girl. To mark his triumph, he outlined a bull in the sky with glittering stars. Since he wanted to show the bull emerging from the sea, only the front half of the animal can be seen. The rest is hidden beneath imaginary waves.

The constellation Taurus contains not only the giant red star Aldebaran, which represents the bull's eye, but two famous subconstellations, the Pleiades and the Hyades. The Hyades, whose name is Greek for "piglets," form the bull's "head." Five in number, they were supposed to be daughters of the Titan Atlas. They mourned for the death of their brother Hyas, who was killed by a wild boar (again the pig motif), and they wept such torrents of tears that the gods placed them in the sky. Through large parts of the world, the Hyades are associated with the coming of the soft spring rains, and the legend of the weeping sisters may be an attempt to explain this. Possibly the Greeks' ancestors sacrificed baby pigs to please the rain-god and make him do his job. Without the rains of spring, the newly planted seeds would not sprout, as even primitive people knew.

The Pleiades, six in number, mark the "shoulder" of the bull. Their name is Greek, but its meaning is rather uncertain. It may mean "many," or "the sailing ones," or "doves." In Greek legend the Pleiades were also daughters of Atlas. In one version, Zeus turned them into stars to save them from the unwelcome attentions of Orion. To enable them to fly up to the heavens, he first transformed them into a flock of doves.

The Arabs were not so romantic about the Pleiades. They called them "The Little Camels." The ancient Jews pictured them as a hen and her chickens.

Although the Pleiades, like the Hyades, signaled the coming of life-giving spring, to many peoples they also symbolized death, for they rose at dawn about the time when the nights became longer than the days. No people took this belief more seriously than the Aztecs, who were obsessed with death in any case. (One Aztec, trying to explain his religion to a Spanish conqueror, said: "We do not believe; we fear.") The Aztecs had a year of 360 days. At the end came five dreaded "empty days." During this period, all fires were put out. No work was done. Everyone fasted. The people sat in their huts and thought fearful thoughts. Just before sunrise on the fifth day, the high priest and his assistants searched the horizon. If the Pleiades failed to rise, the end of the world was at hand. If they did rise, all was well for another year, and they celebrated with a human sacrifice.

In many lands the Pleiades were known as the "seven stars" or the "seven sisters," and there are old traditions that there once were seven. Actually the Pleiades have a faint companion that may have been much brighter in ancient times.

In astrology, Taurus stands for love, beauty, and a soft, yielding nature. It is ruled by the planet Venus. The lucky gem for Taurus is the sapphire; the lucky day is Friday; the lucky numbers are one and nine; and the lucky color is blue. Taureans are said to have attractive, easy-going personalities, but they are apt to let their imaginations run away with them. Taureans are also supposed to be big money-makers or else artistic. William Shakespeare, Presidents Ulysses Grant and James Monroe, and Guglielmo Marconi, inventor of the wireless telegraph, were born under Taurus, along with uncounted millions of other people who never became famous.

Universe

Universe comes from the Latin *universum*, meaning "the whole world" or "everything together." Roman writers created the word from *unus*, "one," plus *versus*, "turned." The universe includes all of space and all that it contains: all the stars, planets, satellites, galaxies, nebulas, comets, and other heavenly bodies, and all the interstellar matter that exists. The universe is so vast that we cannot really imagine it. In fact, the idea of endless space is rather frightening.

Man's early ideas about the universe placed earth at the center of things, with the sun, moon, stars, and planets being guided across the sky by the gods. This, of course, is how it would appear to primitive people with no scientific knowledge but a lot of imagination. Some of the early ideas of the universe seem ridiculous to us today. The Sumerians, for instance, believed that earth was covered by a high dome of metal, the sky. Between sky and earth the heavenly bodies moved along their paths. The Sumerian idea was taken by Babylonians, Egyptians, and other Middle Eastern peoples who added their own variations. The Egyptians thought that the sky was formed by the body of a goddess named Nut, who arched herself protectively over the earth. The Babylonians believed in a series of seven heavens, like the layers of half an onion. The Hindus believed that the universe rested on four elephants who stood on the back of a giant tortoise. What the tortoise stood on was never discovered. The Mayas thought that the universe rested on the back of a crocodile.

Greek astronomers improved on the ideas of earlier civilizations. As early as the fourth century B.C. Greek astronomers thought of earth as surrounded by a series of spheres revolving around it, each one carrying different stars and planets. This theory accounted for the varying motions of sun, moon, planets, and stars. A few Greeks even dared to suggest that the earth was not the center of the universe. Few people believed them.

Early ideas of the universe pictured the earth as flat, like a thick pancake. But as early as 600 B.C. Greek philosophers began to think that earth was spherical. In support of this revolutionary idea they pointed out the fact that a ship's masts sink gradually beneath the horizon as it sails away. They also pointed out the round shadow that earth casts on the moon as a lunar eclipse takes place. But practical men laughed at these theories when they weren't outraged by them.

Around 150 B.C. a Greek astronomer named Hipparchus worked out a system in which the earth was round, but still situated at the heart of the Universe. Around the earth swooped all the heavenly bodies in a complicated network of paths that could be figured out mathematically. About two hundred years later another Greek, Ptolemy, perfected Hipparchus' system. The Roman Catholic Church adopted the earth-centered system of Ptolemy and punished anyone who disagreed with it. A priest named Giordano Bruno was burned at the stake in A.D. 1600 because he insisted on teaching that the earth revolved around the sun and that the stars were other suns. To escape the same fate, the great Galileo was forced to make a humiliating public apology in 1633. He spent the rest of his life under house arrest anyway.

The man who started this furor was a Polish priest named Nicholas Copernicus, who had studied the stars until he could no longer believe the old theories. Copernicus realized that the earth revolved around the sun, instead of the other way around, and that day and night were caused by the earth's rotation. Copernicus did not publish his theories until just before his death in 1543. Considering what happened to Bruno and Galileo, he was wise to be so cautious.

But soon even the Church was forced to accept the new ideas. In the years after Copernicus and Galileo, a German astronomer named Johannes Kepler (1571–1630) and an English mathematician named Isaac Newton (1642–1727) worked out many of the laws governing the motions of the heavenly bodies. As telescopes improved and knowledge of the universe grew, astronomers discovered that the sun was not the center of the universe after all, but just one star in the great galaxy we call the Milky Way. Later it was learned that the Milky Way was only one of uncounted billions of galaxies in space. Yet in spite of the vast numbers of galaxies and stars that exist, they are scattered very thinly through space. For example, the nearest star to our own sun, Proxima Centauri, is 260,000 times as far from us as the sun, and the sun averages just under 93 *million* miles (149.6 million kilometers) from earth. So Proxima Centauri is about 24,180,000,000,000 miles (38,896,000,000,000 kilometers) away. Such a large number, of course, is really meaningless. And the other stars are even further away.

Primitive man and the early civilizations usually thought

that the universe was born when a creator-god separated the sky from the earth or the water of the great World Sea. Today's scientists have different ideas. There are three main theories. All agree that the universe is expanding, that the galaxies are rushing away from each other at speeds of many miles per second.

The big-bang theory holds that the universe began as a dense cloud of hydrogen which exploded violently. The fragments of the cloud condensed into stars, and some of the stars spun off planets and satellites. Ever since the big bang, the universe has been expanding at an ever-increasing rate and will continue to do so.

The steady-state theory holds that the universe has always been pretty much as it is now. While matter is always being destroyed by being turned into energy in the nuclear reactions of the stars, new matter is also being created in the form of hydrogen atoms. New stars and galaxies are constantly forming out of the new matter to take the place of the ones that are moving away. And since space is curved (in their theory, at least), the runaway galaxies will eventually curve back to where they started from.

The oscillating-universe theory holds that the universe began with a big bang, but that the galaxies will eventually slow down in their flight as their energy runs down and the force of gravity begins to exert drag on them. Eventually, gravitational attraction will pull all the stars back together into a dense cloud of matter, and a new universe will be created in a new explosion.

Recent observations from manned spacecraft seem to favor the big-bang theory. But whichever theory is correct, one thing is certain about the eventual fate of the universe. No one alive today will be around to see what happens.

Uranus

Uranus, the third largest of the planets, is named for the mythical Greek Father of the Gods. In Greek mythology, Uranus was one of the very first gods to be created. He was born to Mother Earth as she slept, and later became her husband. Their first children were three giants with a hundred hands each. Next came three cyclops, gigantic, manlike creatures with a single eye in the middle of their foreheads. Then came the Titans, whose name has become a synonym for anything huge and powerful. The story of how one of the Titans, Cronus, overthrew Uranus is told in the entry on PLUTO. Cronus, in turn, fathered Zeus and the other gods of Mount Olympus.

Now, Uranus, in addition to fathering a whole army of giants, was the Sky-God. He symbolized the sky with all its stars and planets. So when a planet beyond Jupiter was discovered in 1781, it seemed only logical to name it for the great Sky-Father, particularly since all the other planets were named for Greco-Roman gods.

Uranus, the first planet to be discovered since ancient times, was found accidentally by an astronomer named William Herschel. Herschel was born in Germany, in 1738, where his father was a musician in an army band. When Herschel was fourteen, he too joined the army as a musician. On the side, he taught himself mathematics. After serving in one of Europe's many wars, he went to England and became an organist at the fashionable resort of Bath. Meanwhile, he became interested in astronomy. Too poor to buy a telescope, he built his own. He even cast and ground the glass for his mirrors (he used a reflecting telescope). One evening he was sweeping the skies with a new telescope when he saw an unfamiliar tiny bright spot in the heavens that was not on any star map. There was no reason for Herschel to suspect the existence of any planet beyond Jupiter, and at first he thought it was a comet. But it did not behave like a comet. In fact, another astronomer showed that it followed the same kind of orbit as a planet. So, after many observations, the discovery of the new planet was hailed, and Herschel became deservedly famous.

The planet Uranus is the seventh planet from the sun. With a diameter of about 32,000 miles (51,000 kilometers), it is a little larger than Neptune and about four times the diameter of earth. But it is a lightweight: Uranus has only 14.5 times the total mass of earth and is just a little denser than water. Its temperature is about $-350°$ F ($-210°$ C), and its atmosphere is composed of hydrogen, helium, and the poisonous gas methane. Uranus shines with a faint, greenish light. On very rare occasions with clear, still air, it can be seen with the naked eye by persons with unusually good eyesight. But most of the time it cannot be seen without a telescope, which is why it was not discovered until Herschel's time.

Uranus lies about 1,800 million miles (2,870 million kilometers) from the sun—about nineteen times as far as earth. It takes eighty-four years to make one orbit. Unlike the other planets, Uranus is tilted so that its axis of rotation is almost at right angles to the plane of its orbit. So the seasons at each pole are forty-two earth-years long. As if to compensate for the lengthy years, Uranus spins much faster than earth, so its day and night are less than half as long as ours. Another odd trait of Uranus is that it rotates in the opposite direction from all the other planets, except Venus. On Uranus, the sun rises in the west and sets in the east. Five moons circle this cold, distant world.

In astrology, Uranus rules Aquarius and controls all unpredictable activities. It is supposed to be a good sign for dealing with railroads and airlines.

Ursa Major

Ursa Major, the "Great Bear," is one of the best-known constellations in the sky. At least, its main part, the "Big Dipper," is the easiest to recognize as its seven stars rotate about the Pole Star night after night.

Ursa is Latin for "bear," and *Major* is Latin for "larger." Why it should have been given this name is a mystery, for it looks nothing like any bear, living or dead. To modern Americans it is clearly a dipper, with four stars forming a bowl and three a long handle. For thousands of years Ursa Major was the same as the Big Dipper, but modern astronomers added a dozen or so extra stars in order to give the "Bear" a head, legs, and paws.

One theory of how the constellation came to be named for a bear goes back to India, perhaps 3,000 years ago. In Sanskrit, the language of the Hindu holy books, there is a word *riksha*, which with different endings can mean either "star" or "bear." "The Seven Stars" is a very old name for the Big Dipper in many lands and many languages. But the Hindu common people confused the Seven Stars with Seven Bears, and later they may have thought the seven bear stars made one Great Bear. Later still, they decided the seven stars were not really rikshas (bears) but *rishis* (wise holy men). So long ago in India the constellation became the Seven Sages. The bears were forgotten, except by a few scholars. Meanwhile, the bear idea had spread west to the Middle East and the Mediterranean lands, where people had to strain their imaginations to invent explanations of how the bear got up in the sky and why it has such a long tail, when real bears have only a stub.

One of the many Greek legends tells that the bear was once a nymph named Kallisto ("the most beautiful"). She had the misfortune to have Zeus fall in love with her. Hera, Zeus' wife, flew into one of her habitual jealous rages and turned Kallisto into a shaggy bear. Not content with this revenge on the innocent nymph, she put Kallisto in a part of the forest where her son Arcas was hunting. Arcas did not recognize his mother; he drew his powerful bow and took aim. In another second he would have pierced her heart—when Zeus saved her by snatching her up to the heavens. In one version, he grabbed the bear by her tail to lift her. She was so heavy that the tail stretched, and this is why the Great Bear has a tail as long as a snake's. Arcas (whose name is a form of "bear") was placed in the sky nearby after his death, as Ursa Minor, the "Little Bear" or "Little Dipper."

Thus did the Greeks explain why they should call the old Seven Stars *Arktos*, "the bear." But they also called them *Hamaxa*, "the chariot." In fact, all through northern Europe, where the Greeks' ancestors came from, the constellation is usually thought of as a wagon. The English used to call it Charles' Wain (an old form of "wagon"). The Dipper does look

170

rather like a crude, old-time peasant's wagon, with the handle forming the wagon's tongue.

Many people also thought it resembled a plow, which is another of the old names for the constellation. The Romans usually called it *Septentriones*, the Seven Plow Oxen. Ancient Chinese astronomers, impressed by the way the Dipper revolves around the Pole Star, concluded that it must be the Jade Balance of Fate, on which the gods of fate weighed the destiny of the world and every living creature. Chinese peasants took a more down-to-earth view of the constellation. They thought of it as a grain measure, where the gods of fate had their palace. To a Chinese peasant, fate meant chiefly whether or not he and his family would have enough to eat the next year. For some strange reason, the God of Literature was also supposed to dwell in the grain measure—perhaps the idea was that you can't write good books on an empty stomach.

The Arabs pictured the constellation as a coffin and mourners. The Coffin (the body of the Dipper) held the corpse of a great warrior who had been slain by the Pole Star. The other stars were the slain man's children, following the Pole Star to seek vengeance.

For some unexplained reason, the ancient Egyptians connected all the constellations in the northern part of the sky with an evil god named Set and his wicked helpers. Set had the head of a hippopotamus or a donkey, and his favorite amusement was bringing suffering upon people. The Egyptians thought the Big Dipper was Set's thigh, and they feared it more than any other constellation.

The Iroquois Indians and many other tribes of the eastern woodlands had a myth about Ursa Major, which they too pictured as a bear. The bear lies sleeping in his den all winter, high in the sky near the Pole Star. In the spring he wakes up and prowls the sky. Three hunters (the three stars of the dipper's handle) pursue him. All spring and summer they circle the sky, until at last the bear's strength fails. The lead hunter takes aim and wounds the bear fatally with his arrow. The blood of the dying bear drips down on earth, turning the leaves of the trees red. The hunters carry off the bear's body and feast on it all winter. But the bear's soul lives on and enters a new body, which again wakes in the spring to be hunted and die with the coming winter.

Since ancient times seamen have used the Big Dipper as an aid to navigation, for the last two stars of the bowl point toward the Pole Star, marking north.

Ursa Minor, the "Little Bear" or "Little Dipper," lies on the opposite side of the Pole Star from Ursa Major. Very conveniently for sky-watchers, the Pole Star is the last star in the Little Bear's "tail"—or in the dipper's handle. Ursa Minor is known mainly for the Pole Star, which the Greeks used to call *Cynosura*, the "dog's tail." Since people were always looking at the Pole Star, the word *cynosure* came to mean something or somebody that was the center of attention, such as a movie star, a professional football player, or a candidate for the presidency.

Vega

Vega is the brightest star in the constellation Lyra. Its name comes from the Arabic word *waqi*, which means "falling." Actually, it is short for "the falling vulture." The Arabs may have gotten the idea that the star was a vulture from a Greek myth about Orpheus, a half-god who was the greatest musician the world ever knew. (He should have been, for his father was Apollo, the god of music.)

According to Greek legend, the lyre was invented by the god Hermes, who found an empty turtle shell on the ground. Having nothing better to do, he stretched strings across the empty shell and began to twang them. To his surprise and delight, he produced musical sounds. After mastering the art of music-making on his new instrument, Hermes traded it to Apollo for a magic staff with wings. Apollo later handed the lyre down to his son Orpheus.

Orpheus traveled around the world as a minstrel, singing and playing for kings and gods. With Apollo's lyre and his own superb voice, he could charm gods, men, beasts, even stones. When his wife Eurydice died, Orpheus followed her to the Underworld and sang so persuasively that even the cold-hearted god Hades agreed to let her follow Orpheus back to earth—provided that Orpheus did not look back at her once during the whole long return journey. Orpheus obeyed this instruction, for he loved his wife deeply. But just as he reached the surface of the earth and stepped out into the sunlight, he turned without thinking to see if Eurydice was following him. Too late he remembered his agreement. Eurydice was lost forever.

Orpheus later died of grief, and Zeus sent a vulture to rescue his lyre and fetch it up to the heavens, where it became the constellation Lyra. The vulture was given a permanent roost among its stars as a reward for service well performed.

Aside from legend, the lyre was one of the favorite instruments of ancient Greece and Rome. It was simple to play; so it was one of the instruments that beginners learned on before graduating to something more complicated. But the lyre also gave its name to a style of poetry, lyric poetry, which began as verses sung to the music of a lyre.

In early Middle Eastern astronomy, long before the Greeks became civilized, Lyra was pictured as a lyre or a harp held in the claws of a vulture. The Greeks must have borrowed this idea for their own myth of Lyra.

Lyra's stars actually form a parallelogram underneath a small triangle. The figure could possibly suggest a bird soaring with some object in its claws, although to a modern person the "lyre" looks more like a slightly squashed cardboard shoebox.

Vega is a very interesting star scientifically as well as to lovers of myth and legend. This brilliant, blue-white star gives off about fifty-three times as much light as the sun, and it is the first star ever to be photographed. (Credit goes to an American astronomer named William Bond, who took its picture in 1850.) The successful photographing of Vega began the era of astronomical photography, which has furnished so much valuable information about the stars.

Thousands of years ago Vega was the Pole Star. In another 12,000 years it will mark the North Celestial Pole once again. Meanwhile the whole solar system is moving toward Vega at twelve miles per second. In some millions of years the Vulture Star may be our neighbor.

Venus

Venus, the second planet from the sun, is named for a leading Roman goddess. Originally, Venus was a rather dim nature spirit, protecting vegetation and crops. Later, she also protected the sewers of the city of Rome. When the simple Roman farmers and warriors came into contact with the Greeks who long ago settled in southern Italy, they confused Venus with Aphrodite, the Greek goddess of sexual desire. So it is that we know Venus best today as the Goddess of Love.

In the early days of Rome, the Romans decided that they needed some important ancestors to win the respect of their neighbors. So they made up a legend that they were descended from a band of refugees from Troy led by Aeneas, who was a Truly Important Person because he was the son of Venus and a Trojan prince named Anchises. Several centuries later, an ambitious man named Julius Caesar was maneuvering his way to dictatorship over Rome and all her possessions. He boldly claimed descent from Venus on both sides. His nephew, the

Emperor Augustus, hired such famous writers as the historian Livy and the poet Virgil to popularize the myth that the blood of the gods flowed in his family's veins. As the official ancestress of the emperor himself, Venus became even more important.

One of the five planets visible without a telescope, Venus was well known to the peoples of ancient times. Shining with a clear, steady yellow glow, it is the brightest of all the planets. At certain times it is bright enough to cast a shadow. An interesting fact about Venus is that it goes through phases like the moon, waxing, waning, and growing dark. It is actually brightest when it is only a thin crescent, since it is much closer to earth then than when it is full. Another odd feature of Venus is that at a certain point in its orbit it seems to slow down, stop, and go backward. This is due to the difference in the speeds of Venus and earth and in their relative positions.

Venus is famed as the Evening Star; at one point in its orbit, it dominates the sky for about three hours after sunset. At a different point, it becomes a morning star, visible for three hours before sunrise. At times it can also be seen in broad daylight (very faintly, if you know exactly where to look).

Because of its brightness and its unusual behavior, Venus was very important to the ancients. The Middle Eastern civilizations identified it with their great goddess of sex and motherhood, who was worshipped under many different names. The Greeks and Romans, who came much later, followed this old tradition. The ancient Jews, with very different religious ideas, identified the bright, wandering "star" with Satan, for as a morning star it seemed to defy the sun as Satan had defied God.

Of course, such an important planet had to have great astrological significance, and the astrologers were ready to fill it in. In modern astrology, Venus rules the constellations Taurus and Libra. It controls love and beauty, and when it is favorable gives peace, happiness, and harmony.

Realistically, nothing was known about Venus until the early 1960s, except that it is almost as large as earth and has nearly the same density. The reason was that the planet is covered by a dense, opaque, yellowish-white atmosphere that no telescope can pierce. In the absence of knowledge, some people theorized that Venus was covered with lush, tropical forests and might even have intelligent life.

In the late 1960s and early '70s the Russians sent several space probes to Venus. Their instruments signaled back that the atmosphere of Venus was about 93 percent carbon dioxide and only one half of 1 percent oxygen. They also showed that the temperature at Venus' surface is nearly 900° F (480° C) and the atmospheric pressure about 90 times that of earth—as great as the pressure 3,000 feet (914 meters) down in the ocean depths.

This put an end to theories about life on Venus, for no form of life imaginable to earth scientists could survive under such extreme conditions. Even the Russians' sturdily built instruments conked out after half an hour. But imaginative writers will probably continue to people Venus with little green men or other exotic beings as long as there are people who like to read about things weird and strange.

Virgo

Virgo, the sixth constellation of the zodiac, was identified by early Christians with the Virgin Mary. The name *Virgo* is Latin for "virgin." But the Virgin is really the ancient Middle Eastern goddess of fertility and sexual love, known under the names of Ishtar, Astarte, and Isis. She was also the Greek Demeter and the Latin Ceres, goddess of grain.

Virgo is always pictured as a young woman carrying an ear of wheat in one hand. This goes back to the time when agriculture was new, and women held the secret of the sprouting and ripening seeds. Although men might be forced to do the heavy work of digging the ground and harvesting, it was the women who had the magic to make the seeds grow and bear. At least, both sexes believed so. The ear of wheat is a reminder that the sun rose among Virgo's stars at harvest time in the ancient Middle Eastern world.

The myths about the fertility goddess all have her descend to the Underworld to search for a dead husband, lover, or child.

179

While she is gone, winter spreads over the earth, and nothing grows. Men and beasts are in danger of starving to death, until the other gods intervene and force the ruler of the Underworld to let the dead one go for part of the year. The return of the goddess and her loved one symbolized the return of spring to the world.

In classical (that is, Greek and Roman) mythology, Virgo was also Astraea, the Goddess of Justice. Astraea lived on earth until mankind became so wicked that she could stand it no longer. She moved to a new home in a better neighborhood—the sky—and her scales of justice became the constellation Libra.

Virgo is a large constellation with no particular shape. It has one notably bright star, Spica, which is one of the twenty-five brightest visible from earth. *Spica* is Latin for "ear of grain," and the star represents the maiden's ear of wheat. Spica is thought to produce about 1,400 times as much light as the sun, but its light takes over 200 years to reach earth.

To the Chinese, who had entirely different myths, Spica was one of the two horns of the Celestial Dragon (the other was Arcturus), and the home of the God of Long Life.

In astrology, Virgo symbolizes chastity and the fulfillment of hope. It is ruled by the planet Mercury. Its lucky gem is sardonyx; the lucky day is Wednesday; the lucky numbers are eight and four (it is curious how often the lucky astrological numbers add up to twelve); and the lucky color is gray (in ancient astrology it was blue speckled with black).

Virgoans are supposed to be intelligent, honest, reliable, realistic, and practical. They are also said to be rather cold and self-sufficient, and very fussy and critical.

Zodiac

Zodiac comes from the Greek name *zodiakos kyklos*, "circle of the animal signs." *Kyklos* is a circle; the English word *cycle* comes from it. *Zodiakos* comes from *zodion*, "little animal," which comes from *zoön*, "animal." Not all of the zodiac's signs are animals—two are human and one is a weighing device—but the great majority are.

If most people were asked to define the zodiac, they would probably answer something like: "That's all those signs that astrologers use to tell your fortune." But the zodiac is much more than that. Scientifically, it is a wide belt of stars on each side of the Ecliptic, which is the sun's apparent path across the sky. (We say the *apparent* path because it is the path along which the sun *seems* to be moving. Actually, it is the earth that is moving.) The zodiac is wide enough to cover the paths of the planets and the moon on either side of the sun's track.

Ancient sky-watchers used the zodiac to keep track of the movements of the planets and the moon as well as the sun. At first it may have had only four points, marking the changes of the seasons: the solstices and the equinoxes. Later, the zodiac was divided into twelve equal parts to match the number of moon-months in the year. These parts are named for the constellations that occupied them in the second century B.C., when the Greek astronomer Hipparchus wrote them down. The twelve signs, as these constellations are called, serve as a kind of heavenly road map.

We say that the sun is "in" a particular sign when the sun lies between that constellation and earth. In this position, the sun appears to rise among the stars of that constellation in the earliest morning. As earth travels around the sun, the sun appears to move from sign to sign. Astrologers believe that the sign in which the sun lies when a person is born has a very great influence on that person's character and abilities. But, because of the precession of the equinoxes, the constellation in each sign is no longer the same as it was in Hipparchus' time. They have shifted one sign backward all around the zodiac. So a person who is born under the *sign* of Aries is actually born under the *stars* of the constellation Pisces. The astronomers' sky-map zodiac, however, still follows the original signs.

The idea of the zodiac probably began with the Sumerians and was borrowed by the peoples who lived later in the Middle East. It spread through the Mediterranean world and east to India. Each people added its own variations, but the main pattern remained the same.

The Chinese had an entirely different zodiac, beginning with the Rat, a "water sign" that corresponds to Aquarius, although with different stars. It went on through the Ox, Tiger, Hare, Dragon, Serpent, Horse, Ram, Monkey, Cock, and Dog, ending with the Pig, which corresponded roughly to

182

Pisces. While the Middle Eastern zodiac runs counter-clock-wise—from west to east—the Chinese zodiac runs in the opposite direction. The reason is probably that the Chinese zodiac was invented to keep track of daily time. Its signs were used to mark the hours (one for each two hours), and also as names for years in a twelve-year cycle ending in a great festival.

There are also lunar zodiacs, which are probably even older than the solar zodiacs, since it is easier to observe the moon's progress across the heavens than the sun's. These moon-based zodiacs have a different constellation for each day of the month, usually twenty-seven or twenty-eight. The Chinese called them *Sieu*, or "Houses," and believed that they represented twenty-eight famous generals of olden times. The Arabs called them *Manazil-al-Kamr*, "Resting-Places of the Moon," for they thought of the moon as pausing in each one to rest, as a caravan stopped to rest each day of its journey. The Hindus called them *Nakshatras*, or star-figures, and in their pictured zodiacs drew houses and beds for the moon to rest in. This is a rather pleasant idea, and with it we end this book.

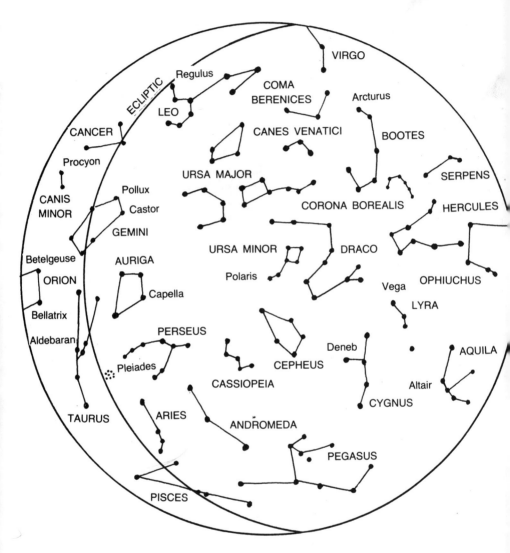

NORTHERN HEMISPHERE

184

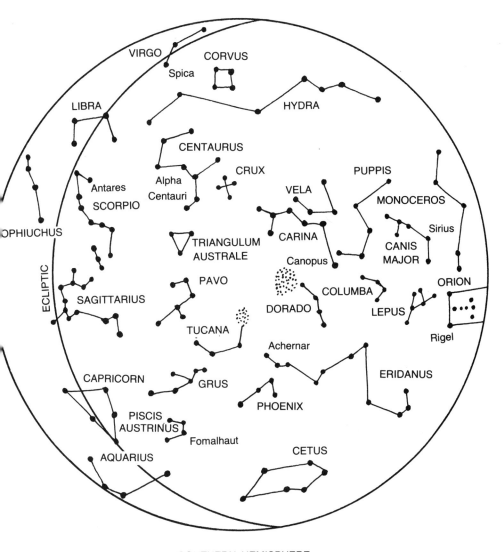

SOUTHERN HEMISPHERE

185

SOME FACTS ABOUT THE PLANETS

	MERCURY	VENUS	EARTH	MAR:
Diameter Miles Kilometers	3,025 Mi. (4,880 Km.)	7,520 Mi. (12,100 Km.)	7,927 Mi. (12,756 Km.)	4,217 (6,787
Density (Water = 1)	5.4	5.2	5.5	3.9
Maximum Distance From Sun (Millions of Mi. and Km.)	43.2 Mi. (69.7 Km.)	68 Mi. (109 Km.)	94.3 Mi. (152.1 Km.)	154.4 (249.1
Minimum Distance From Sun (Millions of Mi. and Km.)	28.7 Mi. (45.9 Km.)	67 Mi. (107.4 Km.)	91.2 Mi. (147.1 Km.)	126.5 (206.7
Period of 1 Orbit (Earth Time)	88 Days	224.7 Days	365.26 Days	687 Da
Rotation Period (Length of 1 Day and Night, in Earth Time Units)	59 Days	243 Days	23 Hr. 56 Min. 4 Sec.	24 Hr. 37 Mi 23 Se
Main Gases of Atmosphere	No Atmosphere	Carbon Dioxide	Nitrogen, Oxygen	Carbon Dioxide
Average Surface Temperature	662°F (350°C) Day −274°F (−170°C) Night	900°F (480°C)	72°F (22°C)	−9°F (−23°C
Force of Gravity at Surface	0.37	0.88	1	0.38
Number of Satellites	0	0	1	2
Color	Orange	Yellow	(Seen From Space) Blue & White	Red

Jupiter	Saturn	Uranus	Neptune	Pluto
88,530 Mi. (142,800 Km.)	76,200 Mi. (120,000 Km.)	32,200 Mi. (51,800 Km.)	30,700 Mi. (49,500 Km.)	3,700 Mi? (6,000 Km.?)
1.3	0.7	1.2	1.7	Unknown
505.7 Mi. (815.7 Km.)	934 Mi. (1,507 Km.)	1,862 Mi. (3.004 Km.)	2,812 Mi. (4,537 Km.)	4,752 Mi. (7,375 Km.)
459.4 Mi. (740.9 Km.)	835 Mi. (1,347 Km.)	1,696 Mi. (2,735 Km.)	2,763 Mi. (4,456 Km.)	2,743 Mi. (4,425 Km.)
11.86 Years	29.46 Years	84.01 Years	164.8 Years	247.7 Years
9 Hr. 50 Min. 30 Sec.	10 Hr. 14 Min.	11 Hr.	16 Hr.	6 Days 9 Hr.
Hydrogen Helium	Hydrogen Helium	Hydrogen Methane Helium?	Hydrogen Methane Helium?	None Detected
−238°F (−150°C)	−290°F (−180°C)	−350°F (−210°C)	−364°F (−220°C)	−380°F? (−230°C?)
2.64	1.15	1.17	1.18	Unknown
14	10	5	2	0
Yellow	Yellow	Green	Yellow	Yellow

Mi. = Miles   Km. = Kilometer   Hr. = Hours   Min. = Minutes   Sec. = Seconds

187

SELECTED BIBLIOGRAPHY

For Science

David Bergamini and the Editors of TIME-LIFE BOOKS. *The Universe*. New York, Time Inc., 1971. A good basic source.

John C. Brandt and Stephen P. Maran. *New Horizons in Astronomy*. San Francisco, W. H. Freeman and Co., 1972. An introductory college text, it is written simply and clearly enough so that many junior high-school readers can understand most of it.

R. Newton Mayall, Margaret Mayall, and Jerome Wyckoff. *The Sky Observer's Guide*. New York, Golden Press, 1971. A good pocket-sized handbook containing basic information about the heavenly bodies.

William T. Olcott. *Field Book of the Skies* (revised by R. Newton Mayall and Margaret W. Mayall). New York, G. P. Putnam's Sons, 1954. Though much of its information is out-of-date, this book contains a good comprehensive treatment of the fundamental principles of astronomy, plus data on the various heavenly bodies.

Among periodicals, *National Geographic, Natural History*, and *Science Digest* give consistently good information on the layman's level. *Science World*'s articles on astronomy are also informative and easy to understand. On a more advanced level, the September 1975 issue of *Scientific American* is a mine of information. It should be noted that new astronomical discoveries are constantly putting existing books on astronomy out of date. The best way to keep up with the latest facts and theories is to follow the newspapers and periodicals.

For Lore and Legend.

Richard Hinckley Allen. *Star Names, Their Lore and Meaning*. New York, Dover Publications, 1963. First published in 1899, this book is not easy reading, but it is crammed with quaint and curious lore.

It seems to be the main source for most later books on star lore.

Sir James Frazer. *The Golden Bough.* New York, Macmillan, 1951. One of the standard sources on mythology.

Robert Graves. *The Greek Myths.* Baltimore, Penguin Books, 1961. The Greek myths briefly and wittily retold, including many little-known but interesting ones. Fascinating explanations of the origins of these myths in the cultures of the Greeks and earlier peoples.

Robert Graves and Raphael Patai. *Hebrew Myths.* New York, McGraw-Hill, 1966 (paperback edition). A similar recounting and interpretation of the Hebrew myths of the Book of Genesis.

Gertrude Jobes. *Dictionary of Mythology, Folklore, and Symbols.* Metuchen, N. J., Scarecrow Press, 1962. An amazing collection of esoteric information.

Maria Leach, editor. *Standard Dictionary of Folklore, Mythology, and Legend.* New York, Funk & Wagnalls, 1949. A more thorough treatment of the same field.

Peter Lum. *The Stars In Our Heaven.* New York, Pantheon Books, 1948. A selection of star legends from all over the world, enchantingly retold.

Anthony S. Mercatante. *Zoo of the Gods.* A witty and informative discussion of the role of animals in legend and myth, with much to say about the stars and constellations. Zolar, *It's All In The Stars.* Greenwich, Conn., Fawcett Publications, 1962. A simple, straightforward introduction to astrology by a well-known practitioner of the art.

For Origins and Derivations of Names.

Richard Hinckley Allen. *Star Names, Their Lore and Meaning. Shorter Oxford English Dictionary.* London, England, Oxford University Press, 1965 edition or later edition.

INDEX

Schiaparelli, Giovanni, 95
Schwassmann-Wachmann II, 57
Scorpio, 23, 60, 92, 121, 148–50
Serpens, 116
Shakespeare, William, 55
Sirius, 11, 121, 151–52
Solar system, 130. *See also* Planets
Solstices, 69, 182
Southern Crown, 140
Spectroscope, 44
Spectroscopy, 43–44
Spica, 180
Sputnik, 143
Star clusters, 13
Star(s), 9–13
  brightness of, 11
  colors of, 11–12, 24
  definition, 9–10
  formation of, 10, 109
  magnitude scale for, 11
  mass of, 12, 24
  sizes of, 10, 12, 24
  temperatures of, 11–12
  See also Novas, Red giants,
  Supernovas, White dwarfs
Steady-state theory, 165
Sun, 10, 42, 63. 69, 153–57, 182; eclipse
  of, 72, 73–74; magnitude of, 11
Supergiants, 24

Supernovas, 115

Taurus, 14, 109, 115, 140, 158–61, 178
Telescope, 42–43; photographic, 44;
  radio, 45, 136
Thuban, 65–66, 113
Titan, 142, 143
Tombaugh, Clyde, 133
Tropic of Cancer, 48
Tropic of Capricorn, 48
Twain, Mark, 57

Universe, 162–65; formation of, 165
Uranus, 26, 110, 129, 142, 166–68
Ursa Major, 28, 169–72. *See also* Big
  Dipper
Ursa Minor, 170, 172. *See also* Little
  Dipper

Vega, 19, 173–75
Venus, 42, 90, 128, 129, 142, 161, 176–78
Vesta, 34
Virgo, 60, 99, 179–80

War of the Worlds, The (Wells), 96
Wells, H. G., 96
White dwarfs, 10, 12, 24, 47, 152

Zodiac, 37, 181–83; Chinese, 182–83

About the Author

Peter Limburg was graduated from Yale University and earned an MA in U.S. history at Columbia University. His fascination with word origins has led him to write five books on the subject for Coward, McCann & Geoghegan including *What's in the Names of Birds* and *What's in the Names of Antique Weapons*.

Mr. Limburg and his wife, Margareta, have four children. They make their home in Bedford, New York.

About the Artist

Carolyn Croll received a BFA from Philadelphia College of Art. She is presently a lecturer there and teaches courses in color and design, form study and children's book illustration. She has illustrated two books for children including *We'll Have a Friend for Dinner*.

Ms. Croll enjoys collecting minatures, doll houses, toys and especially books on Tudor and Victorian England. She makes her home in Philadelphia where she is a member of the Philadelphia Children's Reading Roundtable.